Our Slaughter-house System: A Plea For Reform

C. Cash, Hugo Heiss

GREAT SLAUGHTERING-HALL AT ST. MARX, VIENNA.

(Air—Light—Space, the three desiderata in a slaughter-house.)

OUR SLAUGHTER-HOUSE SYSTEM

A PLEA FOR REFORM

BY

C. CASH, B.A.

TRANSLATOR OF 'HUMANE SLAUGHTERING,' BY HUGO HEISS

AND

THE GERMAN ABATTOIR

BY

HUGO HEISS

LONDON

GEORGE BELL & SONS

YORK HOUSE, PORTUGAL STREET, LINCOLN'S INN

1907

CONTENTS

PART I

OUR SLAUGHTER-HOUSE SYSTEM—A PLEA FOR REFORM

PART II

THE GERMAN ABATTOIR

LIST OF ILLUSTRATIONS

PREFACE

This volume is not the product of a meat scare. Such brief notes and evidence on the slaughter-house question in England as are found in the opening chapters had been already collected, when the sudden exposure of the revolting practices prevalent in the American meat trade called public attention to a subject till then unduly ignored.

The disclosures made were of a nature so pertinent to the subject-matter of this book, and emphasised so strikingly the need which it insists on for controlling and supervising the preparation of flesh foods, that at first it seemed as though some reference to the American meat scandals was unavoidable. Upon consideration, however, it was felt that any plea for reform in this country would come with greater force were it known to have been formulated prior to, and independently of, the terrible object-lesson furnished by the Chicago packing-houses. No reference has, therefore, been made to American meat horrors; but we cannot dismiss the subject without one remark which it seems imperative to make—namely, that the American meat-factory is in no sense an abattoir. The abattoir has, indeed, for its essential object the prevention of those very abuses which have made the American meat-factory a byword in the civilised world.

With regard to the second and more important portion of the book. At the present moment there are various reasons why the Englishman, who has at heart the reform of the slaughter-house system of his own country, should look with special interest to Germany. In England we stand, or it is to be hoped that we stand, on the eve of slaughter-house reform. In Germany that reform is an accomplished fact. It should be interesting, therefore, for us to note by what means and on what lines a change has been carried out in another country which we hope to see effected in our own. As far as the slaughter-house system is concerned, there is much in common between the Germany of thirty years ago and the England of to-day. The evils which called for the introduction of the abattoir system in Germany are the evils which demand a similar remedy in England. The opposition to that system comes from the same quarter, the arguments used for and against it on both sides are the same. But while in England we are only adopting public slaughtering in a tentative and half-hearted fashion—we have abattoirs, but not the abattoir system—in Germany that system has been carried to its fullest development. Those, therefore, among us who are in favour of public slaughtering can point to a country where the experiment has been already tried, and tried successfully. We need not prophesy—we can appeal to facts. Moreover, the example set by Germany has been followed by the leading European States, till at the present moment England stands almost alone in retaining her antiquated system of private slaughter. For the above reasons it has been thought worth while to give a brief history of slaughter-house reform in Germany, and a brief description of the German abattoir as it is to-day—the acknowledged model which other nations have taken as the type to imitate. The author of this portion of the book, Herr Hugo Heiss, Abattoir Superintendent of Straubing in Bavaria, is already known as collaborator with, and literary executor of, the late Dr. Schwarz, author of the great standard work on abattoirs, 'Offentliche Schlacht und Vieh-höfe.' Herr Heiss is also an acknowledged authority on methods of humane slaughtering.

It was originally intended that Herr Heiss's essay should stand alone, but a few preliminary chapters on the evils of the private slaughter-house system in England have been added. That these evils are at length beginning to arouse public attention, there is good reason to believe. During the last few years such events as the appointment of the Commission on

Humane Slaughtering, the American meat scandals, the building of a new abattoir by the Corporation of the City of London, and, finally, the introduction of Lord Donoughmore's Bill in favour of public slaughtering, have all tended to attract the attention of the general public to a question which had hitherto had no interest except for the medical officer and the humanitarian on the one hand, and the slaughterman and meat-salesman on the other.

The aim of this little publication is to enlist the interest of the 'man in the street' in the question. It does not pretend to be a scientific work on abattoirs, but to give in a simple form which may appeal to the ordinary layman some proofs of the evils of the private slaughter-house system, and some description of the advantages of the abattoir. Unfortunately, the subject itself is an unattractive one, and moreover, in framing an indictment of the existing slaughter-house system, it has been found necessary to give as evidence lengthy extracts from official documents, the perusal of which is not an inviting task. In view, however, of the serious question at issue, it is hoped that such drawbacks may be overlooked.

Illustrations of public and private slaughter-houses have been introduced to enable the reader to realise at a glance the striking contrast which exists between the old system and the new.

In this connection the author wishes to acknowledge his indebtedness to Messrs. Beck and Henkel, of Cassel, for the loan of plates illustrating typical German abattoirs.

In conclusion, the author would wish to say a few words with regard to a question which is referred to in this book — the question of adopting more merciful methods of slaughtering cattle. This is a matter on which, unlike the abattoir question, there can be absolutely no diversity of opinion. Everybody who realises the quite needless suffering involved in our present method of killing sheep, pigs and calves, must agree that it is high time that some action were taken in this matter. To those who do not realise what humane slaughtering means as contrasted with the ordinary methods, we may explain that it means the difference between being killed by having a bullet fired into the brain, causing instantaneous unconsciousness, and being killed by having a knife driven into one's throat, and being left to bleed to death. If the choice were given to any one of us, we should, I think, feel quite clear as to which manner of death we should prefer. To the smaller class of animals slaughtered no such choice is given.

It is astounding that in a country where there is so much sensitiveness—we might say, hypersensitiveness—with regard to animal suffering, where, for instance, the law has interfered to prohibit traction by dogs on the score of cruelty, the needless and systematic cruelty of our slaughtering methods should have been ignored. This is not a question of hysterical sentiment, but one on which all sober-minded men with a vestige of humane feeling must think alike. Nor are we speaking on our own authority in this matter. Three years ago a most competent commission, after six months' careful consideration of this question, pronounced its recommendation, 'that all animals be stunned before being bled.' This recommendation up till the present time has remained a dead letter as far as regards its general application, nor have we followed the example of Denmark, Switzerland, and parts of Germany, in making the stunning of cattle compulsory. There is the less excuse for inaction in this matter, because the painless slaughtering appliances invented in recent years have supplied the butcher with a simple and effective means of killing his cattle humanely.

We have dwelt on this question of humane slaughtering at some length, although it may be said that it is not part and parcel of the abattoir question. This may be true; but to our own mind one of the strongest arguments in favour of public slaughtering is, that its publicity affords the surest guarantee that animals will be killed with the least possible suffering. The private slaughter-house is one of the 'dark places of the earth,' and, as we know, it is in such places that cruelty flourishes.

PART I

OUR SLAUGHTER-HOUSE SYSTEM

A PLEA FOR REFORM

CHAPTER I

THE PRIVATE SLAUGHTER-HOUSE

THE average man knows little of the slaughtering systems of his own or other countries. The subject is not one which he has met with in his general reading, nor is he likely to be practically acquainted with it. He has probably never set foot in a slaughter-house since, as a boy, morbid curiosity prompted him to visit one of these 'chambers of horrors' to see a sheep stuck or a bullock pole-axed. If his nerves were not of the strongest, he probably received an impression which has made him shun the sight of slaughtering operations for the rest of his days. And not merely the sight, but the thought of them. He will not allow his mind to dwell upon the subject, and consequently he has never considered it sufficiently to ask himself whether things are managed as they ought to be, or whether there is room for improvement.

Nor is there any literature* dealing with the slaughter-house question which is likely to awaken public interest in it. Apart from the great German work on 'Abattoirs

* This was written before 'The Jungle' had appeared (*vide* preface).

and Cattle Markets,' by the late Dr. Oscar Schwarz, which has been admirably translated into English, but which is somewhat too technical for the general reader, there is no book, so far as we know, which treats of the subject generally. The public press, moreover, is averse to discussing a question of a repellent nature, and even those journals which are devoted to the cause of prevention of animal suffering shrink from dwelling on the forms of cruelty found in private slaughter-houses. In making this statement we except the publications of the Humanitarian League, which has done most excellent work in calling attention to the evils of our slaughtering system.

The general public, therefore, remains ignorant of the subject and indifferent to it because of its ignorance.

The result of such indifference in a country like our own, where reform depends so largely upon public opinion, has been deplorable. Medical officers have protested against the existing state of things on sanitary grounds, and humanitarians have pleaded for improved methods of slaughter, but as yet no real reform has been effected. The slaughter-house system which prevails in England to-day is, in fact, an anomaly and an anachronism—an anomaly because, while we pride ourselves on our regard for sanitary principles, we tolerate a state of things which sets sanitation at defiance; and an anachronism because our system is a crude survival of medieval methods which have been discarded for years past by other European countries.

The slaughtering system which exists, generally speaking, in England at the present day is known as the private slaughter-house system, as opposed to the public slaughter-house or abattoir system.

Under the private system each butcher has his own

private slaughter-house,* situated, as a rule, at the rear of his shop, in which he kills his cattle and prepares the meat for sale. With the public slaughter-house or abattoir system, on the other hand, all slaughtering is done in one or more public slaughter-houses, owned, as a rule, by the municipality, and for the use of which the butcher pays certain dues.

At first sight it might appear that there is nothing very objectionable in the former of these systems.

It is a most convenient arrangement for the butcher to have his slaughter-house close to his shop, and it would appear natural that a man should carry on his private business on private premises. Much depends, however, upon what that business is.

The business of slaughtering is such that there are grave objections to carrying it on in the immediate neighbourhood of the butcher's shop.

These shops are situated, naturally, in the most densely populated parts of our towns, where the butcher is likely to find the readiest sale for his meat, and the slaughter-house is packed away among crowded buildings where its presence is a nuisance and a danger—a nuisance on account of the offensive nature of the work, and a danger on account of the polluting effect of the blood and offal which result from slaughtering operations. Moreover, these private slaughter-houses, which, in view of the nature of the work performed in them, should be models of sanitation, are often quite the reverse.

Any sort of structure is often thought to be good enough for a private slaughter-house, and in many cases these buildings are such that the production of the animal food of the public in them ought to be absolutely prohibited. A statement of this kind, however, requires

* A slaughter-house is often let to other butchers or used conjointly by several men.

to be substantiated, and we therefore give extracts from medical officers' reports referring to the state of private slaughter-houses in different towns. Such extracts are often trying to the reader's patience, but in dealing with a matter of this kind mere assertions, unless supported by independent testimony, are worse than useless.

The report from which it is proposed to first quote is that by the Medical Officer for the City of Coventry in

TYPICAL EXTERIOR OF PRIVATE SLAUGHTER-HOUSE.

1902. It is not with the object of conferring unenviable notoriety on his native town that this report has been selected by the writer, but because in this case he is personally acquainted with the facts, and also because the report brings out so clearly the flagrant manner in which private slaughter-houses contravene existing regulations in regard to their situation, their structure, and their sanitary, or, rather, their insanitary, condition. That this should be the case is not a matter on which the civic authorities can be congratulated, but this subject will be referred to later on.

The report opens by describing what a private slaughter-house should be, and then proceeds to show what many of them actually are.

'Before entering into any particulars as to the character of the existing slaughter-houses, it may be as well to review briefly the characteristics which we expect in a good slaughter-house. A good idea of these characteristics may be obtained from the rules which the Local Government Board have been advised should influence the exercise of the discretionary power of licensing which has been conferred on sanitary authorities.

'These rules are:

'1. The premises to be erected or to be used and occupied as a slaughter-house should not be within 100 feet of any dwelling-house; and the site should be such as to admit of free ventilation by direct communication with the external air on two sides, at least, of the slaughter-house.

'2. Lairs for cattle in connection with the slaughter-house should not be within 100 feet of a dwelling-house.

'3. The slaughter-house should not in any part be below the surface of the adjoining ground.

'4. The approach to the slaughter-house should not be on an incline of more than 1 in 4, and should not be through any dwelling-house or shop.

'5. No room or loft should be constructed over the slaughter-house.

'6. The slaughter-house should be provided with an adequate tank or other proper receptacle for water, so placed that the bottom shall not be less than 6 feet above the level of the floor of the slaughter-house. (This

INTERIOR OF PRIVATE SLAUGHTER-HOUSE.

The flooring of a slaughter-house should be of impervious material, with no crevices to harbour dirt.

is clearly not requisite where a constant supply of water is laid on.)

'7. The slaughter-house should be provided with means of thorough ventilation.

'8. The slaughter-house should be well paved with asphalt or concrete, and laid with proper slope and channel towards a gully, which should be properly trapped and covered with a grating, the bars of which should not be more than $\frac{3}{8}$ inch apart.

'Provision for the effectual drainage of the slaughter-house should also be made.

'9. The surface of the walls in the interior of the slaughter-house should be covered with hard, smooth, impervious material to a sufficient height.

'10. No water-closet, privy, or cesspool should be constructed within the slaughter-house. There should be no direct communication between the slaughter-house and any stable, water-closet, privy or cesspool.

'11. Every lair for cattle in connection with the slaughter-house should be properly paved, drained and ventilated.

'No habitable room should be constructed over any lair.

'In recently visiting the existing slaughter-houses I have borne these requirements in mind, with a view to determining in how many important particulars the slaughter-houses conform to these rules, and in so doing I have grouped them into three classes, according as to whether—

'(*a*) They conformed well;

'(*b*) They failed to conform in some important particular, but were otherwise in good order; or

'(*c*) They failed to conform with several of these rules.

'I think I should be right in describing these three classes as:

'A. Sanitary slaughter-houses.

'B. Insanitary slaughter-houses.

'C. Very insanitary slaughter-houses.

'In the first place, I may say that there is no slaughter-house in Coventry which conforms to rules 1 and 2 in being, and having their fasting-pens, 100 feet from a dwelling-house.

'According to this classification the following is the result of the analysis so made:

A. Sanitary ...	...	...	2
B. Insanitary	...	..	8
C. Very insanitary	...	...	40
Total	...	...	50

'In the following details particulars are given as to the points where these slaughter-houses fail to conform to the requirements of a model slaughter-house.

'Forty are situated in the rear of and in proximity to dwellings; ten are in populated streets in the centre of the town.

'The forty fasting-pens are similarly situated in close proximity to dwellings, except that in seven instances there are no fasting-pens. In six cases they are in a part of the slaughter-house proper, and in one case the stable, fasting-pen, and slaughter-house are one and the same shed.

'In twenty-nine cases the available approach to the slaughter-house is less than 4 feet in width, and in twelve of these it is less than 3 feet. In fifteen cases the entrance forms the right of way to dwelling-houses, while in twenty-three other instances they are the approaches to back premises. In two cases the doors of houses open directly into the narrow passage leading to the slaughter-house.

'Four slaughter-houses have rooms or lofts over them, while one other has a bedroom over it.

'The ventilation in eight cases is bad, in some others it is inadequate.

'The floors should be of impervious material. In fifteen cases the floors may be described as good, in fourteen fair, and in twenty-one others as bad. In one instance the floor consists of a layer of loose bricks laid on the soil.

'In twenty-two cases the drainage is by a gully situated within the slaughter-houses; in three others there is no drainage at all.

'The surface of the walls in the interior of a slaughter-house should be covered with a hard, smooth, impervious material to a sufficient height; in only three instances is this the case. In forty-five other cases the walls are simply brick walls lime-washed, and these cannot possibly be kept in a clean condition, since they cannot be washed. In one other instance the walls are of brick and wood work, while in another they are of wood and galvanized iron. (This last structure is situated in a garden. It has a layer of loose bricks for a floor, no drainage, and no direct water-supply. Its fasting-pen is equally objectionable, and it has the appearance of being a tenant's fixture.)

'In one instance the slaughter-house communicates directly with a stable, in another with a stable and coal-shed, in another with a galvanized iron erection which is used both as a stable and a fasting-pen. In another (already mentioned) the slaughter-house, fasting-pen, and stable are one and the same shed; in another case the stable is in the slaughter-house, and in a further case a horse was stalled in the slaughter-house at the time of my visit. In one case the door of the slaughter-house is within three yards of a public-house urinal and

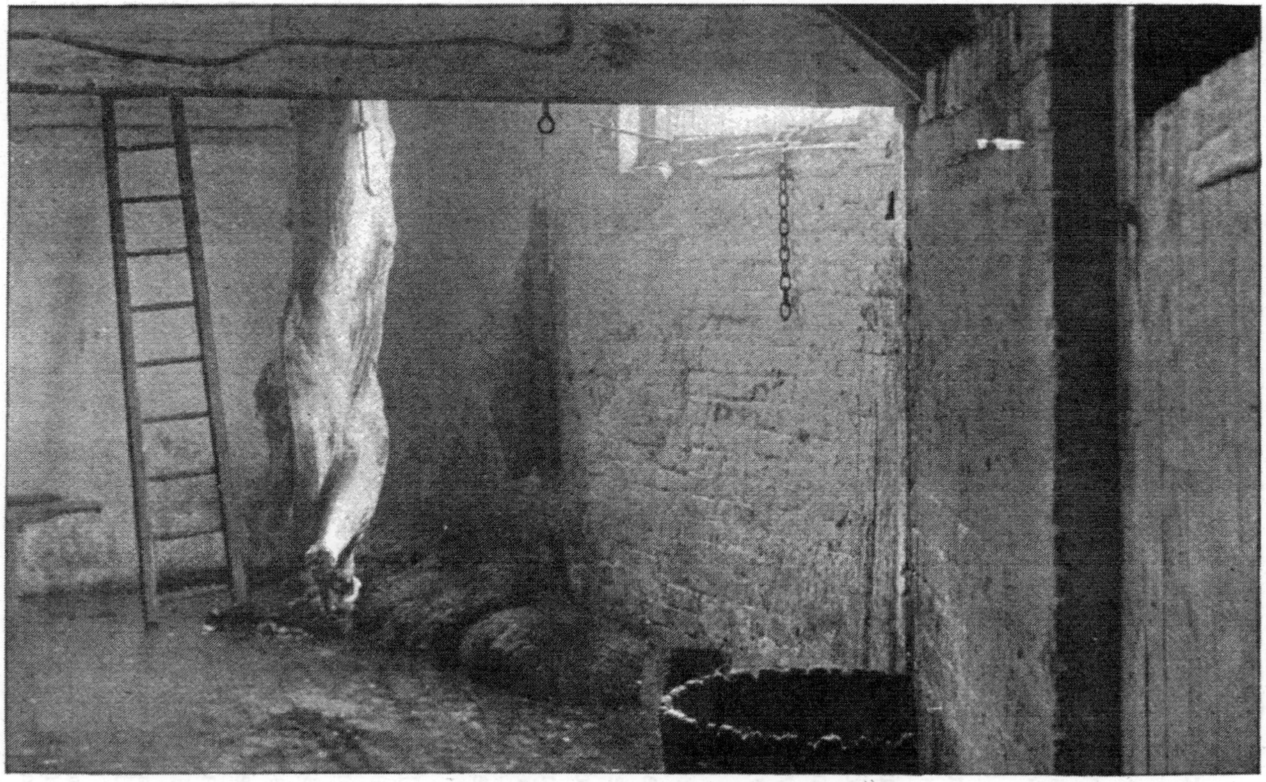

INTERIOR OF PRIVATE SLAUGHTER-HOUSE.

'The surface of the walls should be covered with hard, smooth, impervious material.' Here they are simply brick walls lime-washed.

three water-closets. In two others the door is within $1\frac{1}{2}$ yards of the w.c. door.

'Concerning the fasting-pens, in twenty-one cases the pavement is bad; in twenty-one also the ventilation is insufficient.

'In seventeen instances the yards are badly paved, and in two others there is no paving outside the slaughter-house.

'In one case the slaughtering is always done in the yard, and the slaughter-house itself is used as a sort of chopping-house or bakehouse. In another case the slaughtering was being done in the yard at the time of my visit.

'In thirty-six instances the slaughter-house appears to be used conjointly by two butchers, and in one case by three butchers. If this information be correct, therefore, there are fifty butchers who have slaughter-houses for their own use, or which they could keep for their own use, and there are thirteen others who have no accommodation of their own.

'Conclusions.—It seems hardly necessary to add that the conditions under which our animal food is prepared in this city are anything but satisfactory. How important the safeguarding of these conditions is, has been well brought out by the Medical Officer of Health for Derby in his published report on the recent poisoning cases by pork-pies in that town; and by the poisoning cases themselves that report showed the numerous avenues by which the virulent contamination of food could be effected before it reached the consumer.'*

* With regard to this case of meat-poisoning the following comment appeared in the *Lancet:*

'It seems to us that this case is one more argument in favour of the total abolition of private slaughter-houses. Private slaughter-houses in a large town are nothing but an anachronism, and are always liable to lead to infection of food, cruelty to animals, and in many cases to the sale of diseased or unwholesome meat. The

That the state of affairs described above is in no way peculiar may be seen by a perusal of the annual health reports of other towns. I give the following extracts from a few of these reports taken at random.

In the Annual Report of the Medical Officer of Health for the Borough of Aston Manor for 1903 is the following:

'The number of private slaughter-houses in the borough is twenty-nine. . . . These slaughter-houses are regularly inspected to see that the by-laws are complied with, and to secure, as far as possible, the wholesome character of the meat; but situated, as many of them are, in thickly-populated neighbourhoods, and in the midst of small dwellings, some degree of annoyance and discomfort to the surrounding inhabitants is inevitable, and the provision of a public slaughter-house or abattoir for the town would be a distinct advantage, by encouraging the disuse of these private slaughter-houses, and by rendering practicable a closer supervision over the meat prepared for sale.'

In the Annual Report for 1904 of the Medical Officer of Health for the Royal Leamington Spa is the following:

'I would again bring to your notice that, although the owners and occupiers do their best, I believe, to comply with your regulations, the position and construction of many of the slaughter-houses leaves much to be desired, it being impossible, in many instances, to bring them up to modern requirements; and I trust at no distant date

---

public abattoir, which is open at all times to the inspection of the sanitary authorities, which can be properly drained, and which should be situated at a distance from other buildings, is the only method of ensuring that our meat-supply shall be provided with as little suffering to the animals who afford it, and with as great safeguards of the purity of the meat of those who consume it as is possible.'

PRIVATE SLAUGHTER-HOUSES.

Notice figure of boy in doorway watching slaughtering. An objectionable feature of the private slaughter-house is that the operations can be viewed by children.

In private slaughter-houses the meat is often allowed to cool down in the slaughter-house itself.

Leamington may have a properly constructed public abattoir.'

And again, in the same report, the Inspector of Nuisances says:

'The private slaughter-houses . . . have been kept in fairly good order; two of them, however, are in most unsuitable positions, being converted railway arches. The slaughter-houses and lairage are under one roof and without proper ventilation. The meat is hung up to cool in the same air-space as is used by animals awaiting slaughter. This is most unsuitable, and the only way to overcome the difficulty is to close them, and this course can only be adopted by providing a public abattoir.'

The Annual Report of the Medical Officer of Health for the County Borough of Wigan for 1903 states as follows:

'I can only repeat here that the majority of slaughter-houses are not satisfactory from a public health point of view, or for the preparation of food for man. I hope in the near future we may see a municipal slaughter-house, which will give us every facility for inspection, and also be a fit place for the preparation and storage of flesh meat.'

In the Annual Report of the Medical Officer of Health for the King's Norton and Northfield Urban District for 1903 is the following:

'Some of the older slaughter-houses are very dilapidated, close to houses, and not fit for the purpose. In addition, some are so arranged that the operations can be viewed by children from the outside, an essentially wrong state of affairs.'

Compare also the following letter to the *Daily News*, dated January 15, 1903:

'It is surely time that public attention should be

drawn to the scandalous state of the City slaughter-houses. "Butcher's Row," Aldgate, consists of a ramshackle, tumble-down, irregular block of buildings, the ground floors of which are used as butchers' shops and the upper floors for residential purposes, whilst what in the ordinary course of things would be gardens or backyards have been roofed in by some pre-Adamite carpenter, and are made to serve as slaughter-houses. Take, for example, one which runs alongside "Blood Alley," the narrow court down which the condemned animals are driven to the "lairs" at the rear. One of the slaughter-houses abuts on this, and when I saw it last the operations of the slaughtermen could be easily witnessed by children through a small square window, and a door consisting of iron bars. The place is miserably small and dark, and fitted with the most primitive appliances. I should judge the inside measurement to be about 16 by 13 feet, which would be the size of a small villa drawing-room.

'Some of the slaughter-houses are larger than the one named, but in no single instance can it be said that their construction is at all consistent with modern ideas. The lighting is very bad, and gas has to be used even in the daytime to supplement such light as finds its way in from outside. When we remember that the Corporation of the City of London, which owns these establishments, is one of the wealthiest bodies of the kind in the world, it is indeed extraordinary that such a state should be allowed to exist for a single day.'*

The following extract from Rowntree's 'Poverty' is also instructive:

'There are no less than ninety-four private slaughter-

* Since the above was written the City Corporation has taken a step in the right direction by erecting a new public slaughter-house at Islington.

houses in York. These are too frequently situated in densely-populated, poor districts, often up narrow passages. After slaughtering, the blood is allowed to run into the common sewer, the grates of which are in some cases close to dwelling-houses; the occupants of such houses not unnaturally complain of smells from these open grates. Not a single one of these ninety-four slaughter-houses is built in accordance with the Local Government Board by-laws. Not only is it unsatisfactory for the people to have these slaughter-houses in such close proximity to their dwellings, but their number and situation render adequate inspection all but impossible.'

It may perhaps, however, be thought that the miserable state of the private slaughter-houses described in these reports is unavoidable; that such surroundings are the natural setting of the gloomy work of the slaughterman, and that we must not expect anything better where business of such a kind is carried on.

To dispel such an utterly false idea, compare for one moment the arrangements of the splendid slaughtering-halls found in German abattoirs, photographs of which are given on pp. 151 and 153.

These halls, sometimes as much as 30 feet high, airy, and well lighted, are constructed with the greatest regard for sanitation. The flooring is of carefully-chosen materials—stone slabs or flags so closely fitted together that no interstices remain to harbour dirt. The walls, faced with glazed tiles or even white marble up to a certain height, are kept spotlessly clean, and it is expressly forbidden to use red paint in any part of the slaughtering-halls, so that splashes of blood may not be concealed by the colour. In short, the minutest care is taken in every detail to ensure the most absolute cleanliness. And we English people, who pride ourselves, above all, on our superiority to the foreigner

PRIVATE SLAUGHTER-HOUSES.

Compare confined space in which slaughtermen are crowded with roomy slaughter-hall of an abattoir.

Primitive arrangements for scalding pigs. Contrast with plate, p. 177.

in point of cleanliness, are content to have our flesh food prepared in wretched ramshackle buildings, saturated with dirt and offensive matter. As long as the butcher's shop is smart and trim, we do not trouble to look behind the scenes.

The reader will best realize the contrast between our own system and that in vogue abroad from a glance at the accompanying photographs of typical English private slaughter-houses and some of the slaughtering-halls found in abattoirs on the Continent.

CHAPTER II

MEAT INSPECTION

We have spoken of the objections to private slaughter-houses on the ground of their sanitary defects and unsuitable situation. We have next to consider what is, in fact, a far more serious objection, and one which concerns, not the individual slaughter-house, but the whole system collectively. Were each private slaughter-house, in its construction and appointments, equal to the best-built abattoir, this objection would still hold good. It consists in the impossibility of proper meat inspection when cattle are slaughtered in a number of different slaughter-houses scattered over a large area. How is it possible, indeed, for two, or perhaps three, sanitary inspectors, who have many other duties to perform, to visit, let us say, fifty different slaughter-houses, situated at considerable distances from each other, and inspect every freshly-killed carcass before the meat is offered for sale?

Slaughtering often takes place on one and the same day in any town, and it is physically impossible for the inspectors to examine meat killed at fifty or more different places in one day. Consequently, unless a perfect army of inspectors be employed, there can be no effective meat inspection.

In the city of Bristol, for instance, there were in 1904

112 private slaughter-houses, and when, at the beginning of that year, one of the sanitary inspectors was questioned as to meat inspection in the city, he replied that there was 'great need for public abattoirs in Bristol, inasmuch as it was impossible for two inspectors to examine all animals that were killed in the city.'

Dr. Davies, the Medical Officer for Bristol, also stated, in reference to the large number of tuberculous pigs whose carcasses were seized in the last six months of the year 1903, that 'the report of the chief inspector disclosed a very serious state of affairs of grave import to the city, in which the arrangements for securing adequate inspection of the meat-supply were, with 112 scattered private slaughter-houses, about as bad as they could be.'

Compare also the report of the Public Health Committee of the London County Council in 1898. The report states:

'(*a*) That, in the opinion of the Council, it is desirable that, as a first step towards ensuring the proper inspection of meat, private slaughter-houses should cease to exist in London, and that butchers should in substitution be afforded such facilities as are necessary for the killing of animals in public slaughter-houses to be erected by the Council.

'(*b*) That a copy of this report and of the Council's resolution thereon be sent to the Local Government Board, with an intimation that the Council is prepared to accept such responsibilities as may be necessary to give effect in London to the recommendations of the Royal Commission on Tuberculosis, and that the Board be asked whether they will include in any legislation introduced by them in connection with the Royal Commision's report the provisions which would be necessary for this purpose.'

The Council, however, owing, no doubt, to the powerful opposition of the Meat and Cattle Trade Associations, has shelved the matter for the present.

Again, take the following statement by Dr. E. P. Manby, Medical Inspector to the Local Government Board, and late Assistant Medical Officer of Health at Liverpool. Concerning private slaughter-houses he says:

'It is obvious to anyone how inefficient meat inspection must be where there are a large number of private slaughter-houses in a town. The occupiers naturally slaughter at times to suit their own convenience, and not that of the inspector. In Liverpool, with a population of 668,000, we have, besides an abattoir owned by a private company, only thirty private slaughter-houses, and we have five meat inspectors, who devote their whole time to the work. But in smaller places, where there are, perhaps, many more slaughter-houses and no special inspectors, meat inspection becomes very often practically a dead-letter. One remedy suggested for this state of things is to increase the number of meat inspectors as being cheaper than closing all private slaughter-houses and building municipal ones. Cheaper it would be, of course, and better than the present conditions, but how far behind the methods adopted, for example, in Germany! And even if, as has been suggested, one inspector to every ten slaughter-houses be appointed, the question of insanitary conditions under which slaughtering takes place in many private slaughter-houses would not be remedied, though it might be improved.'

Compare also the Annual Report for 1903 of the Medical Officer of Health for the County Borough of Stockport, which contains the following:

'Effectual supervision is rendered almost impossible from the fact that the places are scattered over a large area, and that slaughtering is done at most irregular and untimely periods.'

Again, in the report for 1904 the Medical Officer of Health for King's Norton, and Northfield Urban District, speaking of meat inspection, says:

'How can this be carried out unless inspection of the slaughtering is possible? In order that meat inspection can be carried out thoroughly a public slaughter-house is absolutely necessary.'

In the report for the borough of Torquay in 1904, it is stated that 'the fact of having so many private slaughter-houses, and also that a considerable amount of meat is brought in from a distance by train, renders the proper inspection of meat impossible.'

And in the report for East Ham for 1902 the medical officer remarks:

'The primary object of meat inspection is the detection of danger to the consumer of meat offered for sale; its secondary objects are the protection of the public against imposition and fraud, and to aid in the suppression of diseases which are transferable from animal to animal; and I should very much like to see the establishment of a public abattoir and meat depot, for without such no effective control of the meat-supply is possible.'

The following is also important, being an extract from the Annual Report on the Health and Sanitary Condition, etc., of the Parish of St. Mary Abbotts, Kensington, for the year 1898, by T. Orme Dudfield, M.D.:

'In connection with the subject of slaughter-houses, reference may be made to an instruction by the County Council to the Public Health Committee to report as to the desirability of establishing public slaughter-houses throughout London, and as to the facilities which such a system would afford for the better inspection of the meat-supply. The medical officer of the Council submitted a report on the subject, in which he showed the inadequacy of the inspection of meat consumed in London, and pointed out that diseased meat was largely received into London, and that for protection, especially of the poorer inhabitants, who are the purchasers of the cheaper meat, it was necessary that a system of inspection of all dead meat introduced into London, and which had not been examined in a public slaughter-house, should be instituted. In order, moreover, to ensure the inspection of meat killed in London, he considered it necessary that all animals should be killed in public slaughter-houses, in which alone due inspection of the meat is practicable. By far the greater number of such animals are killed in the slaughter-houses of the Corporation of the City of London, at Deptford and Islington; but information obtained from occupiers of private slaughter-houses, of which there are some 438 in London (as compared with 1,500 in 1874, when the now repealed Slaughter-houses Act was passed), showed that in winter some 900 beasts, 7,000 sheep, and 900 pigs, and in summer some 800 beasts, 11,000 sheep, and 500 pigs, are killed per week in these parishes. The Committee in their report (July 21) stated that the systematic inspection of the animals is impossible in view of the numerous premises in which they are killed.'

Finally, let me quote from the report on the city of Coventry in 1902. Dr. Snell says:

'The systematic inspection of meat cannot be said to exist in this city; it would be an utter impossibility while the slaughtering is effected in fifty scattered slaughter-houses. Some butchers report to the Health Department whenever they have a carcass which does not appear sound. In most cases this leads to the condemning and confiscation, without any compensation, of meat found to be diseased. Unless so reported, it would be only the barest chance that it could be discovered. It follows that it is the honest butcher who has to pay the penalty for his honesty.'

The above extracts are, I think, sufficient to prove the impossibility of efficient meat inspection with the private slaughter-house system. On the necessity for such inspection I need not insist. The subjoined footnote, describing meat-poisoning epidemics which have periodically occurred, is ample evidence on this point.*

I have no intention here of entering into the pathological problems involved in a discussion of the varying transmissibility of different diseases of animals to man through the eating of meat. It is sufficient for our present purpose to recognise that various diseases are so transmitted, and that the boiling, roasting, or pickling of meat affords but an imperfect protection against this transmission.

The most serious of these transmissible diseases consist of those depending on the existence of animal parasites, such as trichina and tapeworm; and those of an infectious or toxic nature, such as tuberculosis, glanders, anthrax, rabies, septicæmia, pyæmia, and meat-poisoning.

Some of the conditions which render meat unfit for food may be apparent to the buyer. If this were always the case the necessity for a skilled inspector would not exist; but, unfortunately, the most dangerous conditions

* In a recent address given by Dr. Geo. Newman, Medical Officer for Finsbury, it was stated that, since the occurrence of the 'Welbeck disease,' in June, 1880, there have been not less than fifty somewhat similar epidemics of ptomaine-poisoning shown to be due to infection through such food as pork-pies, boiled hams, tinned meats, etc. The outbreak at Mansfield, in 1896, affected 265 persons; and that at Derby, in 1902, 220 persons. Nor was it alone in epidemic form that 'food-poisoning' made its appearance. Every year the bills of mortality told a story of deaths from such causes.

are those which are not so apparent. The casual purchaser is entirely unprotected; in many cases the butcher himself may be without the slightest suspicion that his meat is not of the best. This being so, it is impossible to deny that the expert inspection of all meat before sale is extremely desirable from the point of view of the purchasing public.

The desirability of this has been recognised from the earliest times. The Mosaic laws relating to what meat could be eaten and what could not will be recalled. The Athenians had a system of market police. In Rome, from the earliest times, ædiles were appointed to control the meat markets. As early as A.D. 164 butchers were punished because they sold meat which had not been inspected by the authorities.

In Germany, from the time of the Middle Ages, some form of systematised meat inspection has existed. The thoroughness of the present methods are set out fully in another portion of this book by Herr Heiss.

A general regulation of meat inspection is found at the present time also in the following civilised countries: Belgium, France, Holland, Spain, Italy, Austria-Hungary, Roumania, and Switzerland.

It is a matter for considerable reflection that in this country, which prides itself on its hygienic advancement, there is no general and systematised inspection of meat.

With regard to the legal aspect of the question, we may mention that the statutory provisions enabling meat inspection to be carried out in this country are contained in Sections 116 to 119 of the Public Health Act, 1875, and Section 28 of the Public Health Acts Amendment Act, 1890. These sections give power to a medical officer of health or an inspector of nuisances to inspect and examine any article intended for the food of man, and determine the method of procedure if such article is not considered to be fit for human consumption.

These provisions are important, but they are a long way from rendering the establishment of a systematic inspection of meat possible. Other things are necessary. It is necessary that the slaughter-houses should be few in number, in order that it may be possible for a reasonable small staff of inspectors to be present whenever slaughtering is going on, and so to ensure the examination of all meat.

All inspectors who are entrusted with the duty of meat inspection should be properly trained in their duties; a sound opinion on the fitness or unfitness of meat for food can only be expressed by one who has had a thorough training in meat inspection. In this country, outside of London, it is open to sanitary authorities to appoint anyone to the post of inspector of nuisances. He may be totally ignorant of anything pertaining to sanitary matters; he may be quite innocent of any knowledge concerning the nature of the duties he is to be called on to perform; he may know absolutely nothing about food inspection. The only thing necessary is that his appointment should commend itself to the local authority. The confirming of the appointment by the central authority generally follows as a matter of course. Even to-day such appointments are made, and our habit, as a country, of priding ourselves on our sanitary advancement, as compared with other countries, remains unshaken.

The question is sometimes raised as to whether the inspector of meat should be a veterinary surgeon or a sanitary inspector. It does not appear necessary to argue much on this point until the preliminary one of the systematic inspection of meat is determined. Much may be advanced in favour of always employing a veterinary surgeon, provided he has had included in his curriculum of education a training in this particular matter. A sanitary inspector who has gone through a course of such training and an accredited examination may be for all practical purposes an efficient inspector. Probably the determining point will be that of expense, the larger towns, with extensive slaughter-houses, employing the former, and the smaller ones the latter.

It may perhaps be of interest to give the following extract as bearing on the question. It is from a report of the Royal Commission appointed to inquire into the administrative procedures for controlling danger to man through the use as food of the meat and milk of tuberculous animals.

The report states that—

'There is a total absence of uniformity in the special qualifications required of the persons employed as meat inspectors by the sanitary authorities in different places, as may be seen by a return presented to the House of Commons in 1896, showing the previous vocations of those acting in that capacity. In Battersea, for instance, four plumbers and three carpenters discharged the office of meat inspector; in Hackney the duties have been committed to two plumbers, one carpenter, one compositor, one bricklayer, one florist, one builder, one surveyor, and one stonemason. In Portsmouth a solitary butcher has received as colleagues three school teachers, one medical dispenser, one carpenter, and one tram-conductor.'

The report adds that 'A number of witnesses expressed the opinion that veterinary inspectors alone should be employed. On this question we are satisfied that some pathological training is the proper basis upon which to build the knowledge required by a meat inspector, and that, wherever practicable, veterinary surgeons, thus educated, should be employed as meat inspectors. In large towns, where a staff of inspectors is maintained, we do not think it necessary that all of these should be veterinary surgeons, but all meat inspectors should pass an examination and receive a qualifying certificate from a central authority before appointment.'

Compare also the following recommendation as to the qualifications of meat inspectors by the Commission:

'We recommend that in future no person be permitted to act as a meat inspector until he has passed a qualifying examination, before such authority as may be prescribed by the Local Government Board (or Board of Agriculture), on the following subjects:

(*a*) The law of meat inspection, and such by-laws, regulations, etc., as may be in force at the time he presents himself for examination.

(*b*) The names and situations of the organs of the body.

(*c*) Signs of health and disease in animals destined for food, both when alive and after slaughter.

(*d*) The appearance and character of fresh meat, organs, fat and blood, and the conditions rendering them, or preparations from them, fit or unfit for human food.

CHAPTER III

PUBLIC SLAUGHTERING A SAFEGUARD AGAINST CRUELTY

BESIDES the impossibility of effectual meat inspection there is, however, another evil which results from the want of proper supervision under the private slaughter-house system. That evil consists in the absence of the check on cruelty which publicity or supervision affords.

The work of slaughtering is done in private often even without the slaughterman's employer being present. The sanitary inspector is rarely there, and officers of the Society for the Prevention of Cruelty to Animals have no right to demand admission to private premises.

We need not insist on the opportunities for undetected acts of cruelty which such a state of things admits of.

Butchers naturally resent the imputation that they are cruel as a class, merely because it is part of their work to slaughter cattle. Quite so. Nor are our carters and cabdrivers cruel as a class, and yet in 1904 there were upwards of 5,000 convictions for cruelty to horses alone. Of convictions for cruelty in slaughtering operations there was not a single instance.* Does this mean that not a single act of brutality was perpetrated in any

* In 1905 the only conviction for cruelty in slaughtering was in the case of two calves being slowly bled to death. The convictions for cruelty to horses amounted to about 5,000.

slaughter-house, or that, owing to the privacy in which the work of slaughtering is done, no such act was detected?

But not only is there opportunity for incidental cruelty under the private slaughter-house system: there is also inherent cruelty in our methods of slaughter themselves. By cruelty we mean the infliction of avoidable suffering. The butcher may say, 'I inflict no avoidable suffering. I cannot slaughter without inflicting pain.' This is exactly the point where we join issue with him. If an animal be stunned or otherwise rendered unconscious before blood is drawn, its death is rendered relatively, if not absolutely, painless. And no valid argument has yet been brought against this position.

The animal bleeds equally well whether it has been stunned or not, and the fact that the butcher stuns his bullock—not, however, from motives of humanity, but because of the difficulty of controlling a large and powerful animal—proves that he has no objection to the practice.

The various appliances which have been invented in recent years for stunning animals, such as 'Greener's Humane Cattle-killer,' and the German slaughtering-pistol, described on page 172, leave the butcher who is really humane little excuse for slaughtering in the old and barbarous way.

Of recently-invented slaughtering appliances the writer may speak with some authority, having made a study of this matter during the last three years. A model slaughter-house was built by the author's brother some three years ago, and in this experiments and demonstrations with what is probably the most approved German slaughtering appliance—namely, Behr's pistol—have been most successfully carried out. Local butchers who have been induced to use the contrivance

CHICAGO PORK-FACTORY.

Pigs hung up alive by the hind-legs, and stuck while in this position No stunning.

speak highly of it, and it is to be hoped that both this apparatus and the 'Greener' may be generally taken up. Of these two, the 'Greener' seems best adapted for large animals, and the Behr pistol for pigs, sheep, and calves, for the following reasons: In the 'Greener' apparatus a bullet is used, which has great penetrative power, but which may be dangerous if the animal's carcass is not sufficiently bulky to preclude the possibility of the bullet passing clean through it. With Behr's pistol the bullet is replaced by a bolt, which never leaves the pistol barrel, but is driven into the animal's brain by the charge and then automatically withdrawn.

We have pleasure in stating that the 'Greener' is in use in the following abattoirs and leading slaughter-houses:

Aberdeen.	Gateshead.	Paisley.
Arbroath.	Glasgow.	Rugby.
Barnsley.	Hartlepool.	Scarborough.
Bath.	Hull.	Sheffield.
Belfast.	Inverness.	Sherborne.
Birmingham.	Leeds.	Singapore.
Bristol.	Leicester.	Stafford.
Cairo.	London.	Stirling.
Carlisle.	Manchester.	Sunderland.
Cheltenham.	Newcastle.	Swansea.
Durban.	Nice.	Worcester.
Edinburgh.	Northampton.	York.

The 'Greener' has also been issued by the War Office for use in the Butchery Department, Remount Department, in Transports, and in the field. A full description of Behr's pistol will be found on page 172.*

* The author begs to state that he has no interest other than humanitarian in either the 'Greener' apparatus or Behr's pistol.

STUNNING BULLOCK WITH 'GREENER.'

SLAUGHTERING PONY WITH 'GREENER.'

I need not recall the fact that the whole question of humane slaughtering was investigated two years ago by a Committee sitting at the Admiralty under the very able chairmanship of Mr. Arthur Lee, M.P. This Committee dealt with the subject most thoroughly, taking expert evidence and witnessing practical experiments, and finally pronounced its verdict in the recommendation that 'all animals be stunned or otherwise rendered unconscious before blood is drawn.'

The Committee also expressed itself strongly in favour of public abattoirs in preference to private slaughter-houses.

'In the interests not only of humanity, but of sanitation, order, and ultimate economy, it is highly desirable that, where circumstances permit, private slaughter-houses should be replaced by public abattoirs, and that no killing should be permitted except in the latter, under official supervision. Such a change as this could only be brought about gradually and by legislation; but it cannot be described as impracticable, in view of the fact that this system is prescribed by law in several Continental countries, and is actually enforced in the city of Edinburgh.

'There should be an efficient system of inspection and supervision of all slaughter-houses, whether public or private, by the local authority, and uniformity in methods of slaughter should be introduced and enforced as far as possible.'

There can be no doubt that this question of humane slaughtering is a matter for legislation. The law as it stands is an anomaly. We have the most minute and explicit regulations for the care of cattle in transit. On its way to the slaughter-house the animal, theoretically, has every attention paid it. There must be no overcrowding; there must be a sufficient supply of food and water; the floor of the truck in which it travels must be so constructed that it cannot slip and injure itself. But at the door of the slaughter-house the law is silent. The animal has come under the jurisdiction of the municipal by-laws which control and regulate the private slaughter-house.

These by-laws are framed at the discretion of each

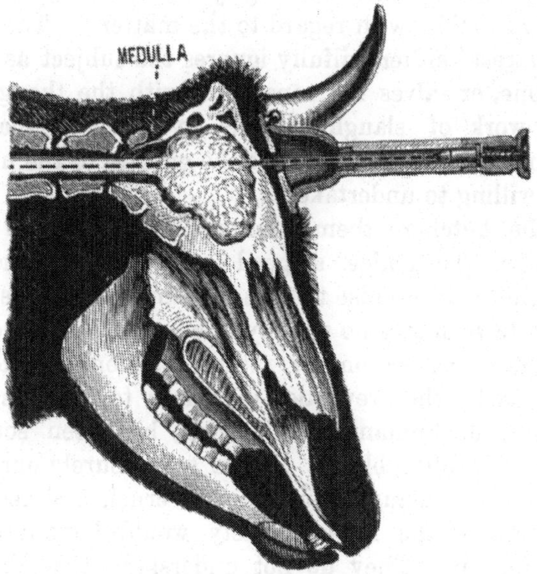

'GREENER' APPARATUS.

Section of bullock's skull.

municipality, upon the lines of the model by-laws for slaughter-houses drawn up by the Local Government Board. In these model by-laws there is indeed a clause recommending vaguely the avoidance of cruelty, but no stipulation that animals shall be stunned before being bled.

A step in the right direction would be made if such a

clause were inserted, but even then it would be optional for each municipality to embody such a clause in its own regulations or to omit it, as seemed good. How much more satisfactory it would be were a short Act of Parliament framed, making it universally compulsory to stun animals before using the knife!

That at present so little has been done to reform our slaughtering methods is largely due to the apathy of the general public with regard to the matter. 'The man in the street' either wilfully ignores the subject as a painful one, or salves his conscience with the thought that the work of slaughtering is so repellent that some license in their methods must be granted to the men who are willing to undertake it.

The butchers themselves will take no lead in the matter. To oblige a good customer the individual butcher will promise to stun his animals, but as a class they have shown no anxiety to adopt humane methods.

Again, the action, or rather inaction, of the Royal Society for the Prevention of Cruelty to Animals, in this matter of humane slaughtering, has been something of a stumbling-block. People say, 'Surely our present methods of slaughtering are not cruel, and require no reform, or the Royal Society would have taken the matter up.' They do not understand that the Royal Society confines itself to supplementing the work of the police by bringing offenders against existing laws to book, and does not attempt to initiate reform in the law itself. Whether the Society might not use its influence in this direction with advantage is not for me to say.

I merely note that the late Clare Sewell Reade, before writing those letters to the *Times* which resulted in the appointment of the Humane Slaughtering Commission, appealed to the Royal Society to move in the matter, but without result.

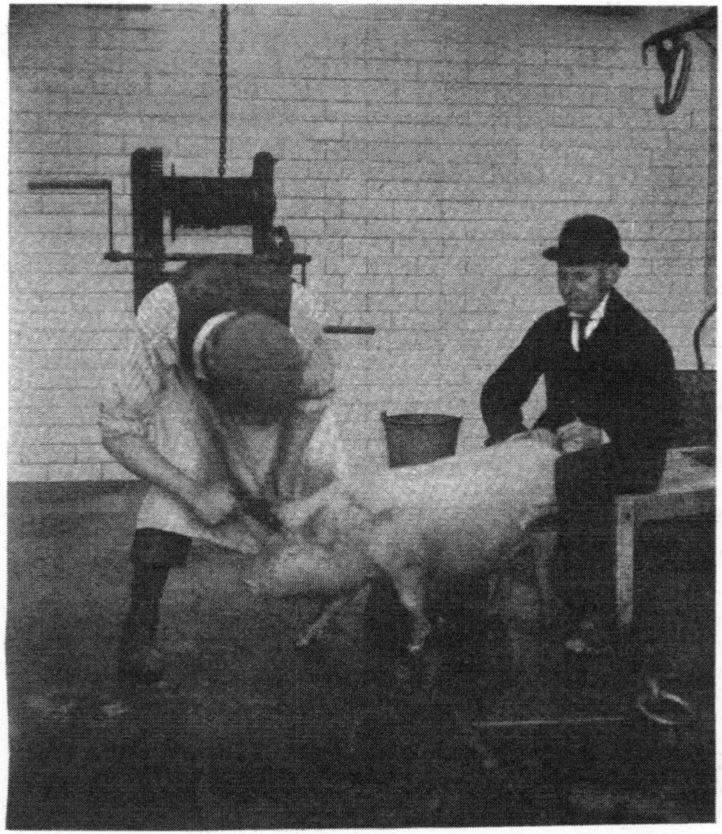

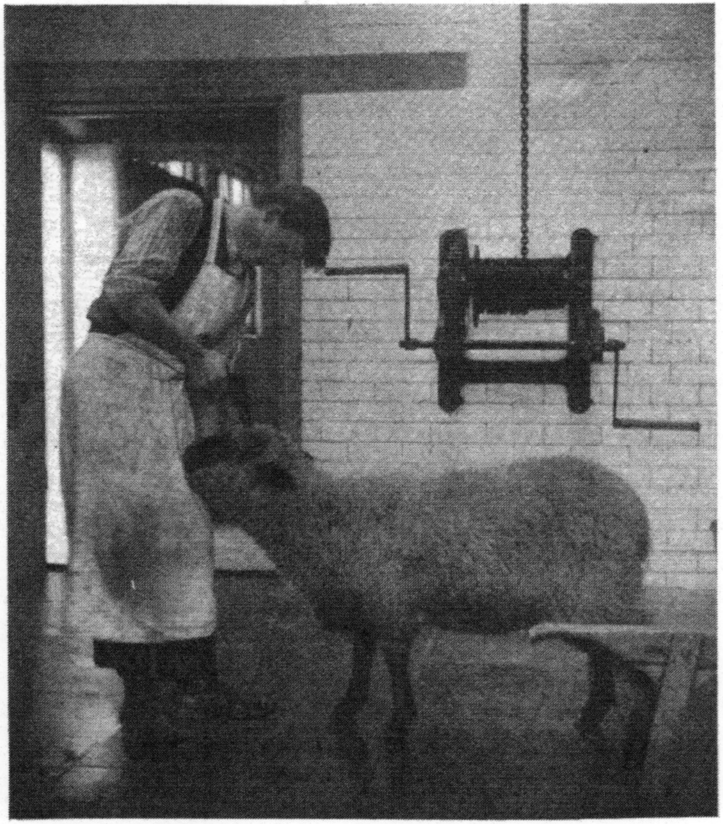

STUNNING CATTLE WITH BEHR PISTOL.

Note absolute safety of apparatus. No danger of bullet striking anyone present.

In stunning sheep with Behr pistol, no need to tie legs or hold animal down.

That the Royal Society realises the evils of the private slaughtering system on humanitarian grounds is obvious from the following passage which appeared in the Society's annual report for 1904:

'In the large London butcheries the slaughterers are employed solely in killing, and thus become efficient and skilful. Generally the various parts of the work are allotted to and performed by the most perfect hands—particularly the stunning process. So far, therefore, as dexterity and experience are concerned, it would appear reasonable that less suffering to the animals is caused in large than in small slaughter-houses. In these houses the operators may not be less efficient, but are less under surveillance. Situate, as these places sometimes are, at the rear of a dwelling-house, or away from the master's eye in a distant yard, working butchers often perform their calling unseen by anyone. Intruders are warned off as trespassers, and officers of the Society may be forbidden admittance. The shed is private "property," and open only to the very rare visit of a sanitary inspector. It need surprise no one that under such conditions brutality often flourishes unchecked. In the large houses alluded to a master slaughterman or foreman is present to prevent the excesses of young and reckless persons; and in abattoirs there is not only an inspector, but the public eye, to deter workmen from cruelty. An inference in favour of abattoirs, therefore, is easily drawn.

'The erection of public abattoirs in place of private slaughter-houses secures better sanitary conditions; better inspection as regards the treatment of animals; better means of preventing beating, tail-twisting, and other forms of cruelty when animals are conducted through doorways or passages; better skill in the necessary operations of slaughtermen, as well as means for testing alleged better methods of slaughtering, which cannot be obtained in private slaughter-houses. Terror-stricken beasts, instead of being forced by sheer violence

ORDINARY METHODS OF SLAUGHTERING.

Sheep killed with knife, without being stunned. Calf hung up alive, and slaughtered by cutting throat. No stunning.

through overcrowded carriage-ways, will repose in roomy lairs until the moment of death arrives, thus their flesh will remain unfevered; instead of the concealed cruelty that occurs in small private slaughter-houses, where inefficient men and lads go through their daily avocations unrestrained by inspectors, there will be capacious and convenient appointments, where over-crowding will be impossible, where every application that science can devise for speedy death will be in use, where inspectors will be provided to prevent abuses, and where, consequently, workmen of humane character and superior skill will be employed.'

One word, in conclusion, in reference to the delicate question of the Jewish method of slaughtering which forbids stunning.

For those who are unacquainted with the process, it may be well to explain that the 'Schechita,' or Jewish mode of killing oxen, consists in 'casting' or throwing the animal to the ground, forcing the head back, and cutting the throat. The animal expires from loss of blood, of course, without having been previously stunned.

As I write I have before me the January number of the German *Tierfreund* for 1906, containing a report on this very subject in the form of answers to twenty-five questions addressed to abattoir directors all over Germany.* I cannot refrain from expressing admiration for the thoroughness with which this report has been drawn up, and also for the absence of that squeamishness which makes English journals shrink from the discussion of an important subject because it is a painful one.

The evidence contained in this report against the Jewish method of slaughtering on humanitarian grounds is overwhelming. The 'Schechita' is condemned as barbarous on account of the cruelty involved in the 'casting' process and the omission to stun. But—and the saving clause is a weighty one—the 'Schechita' is a religious rite regarded as essential by every Jew who is

* The exact number of abattoirs applied to was 585.

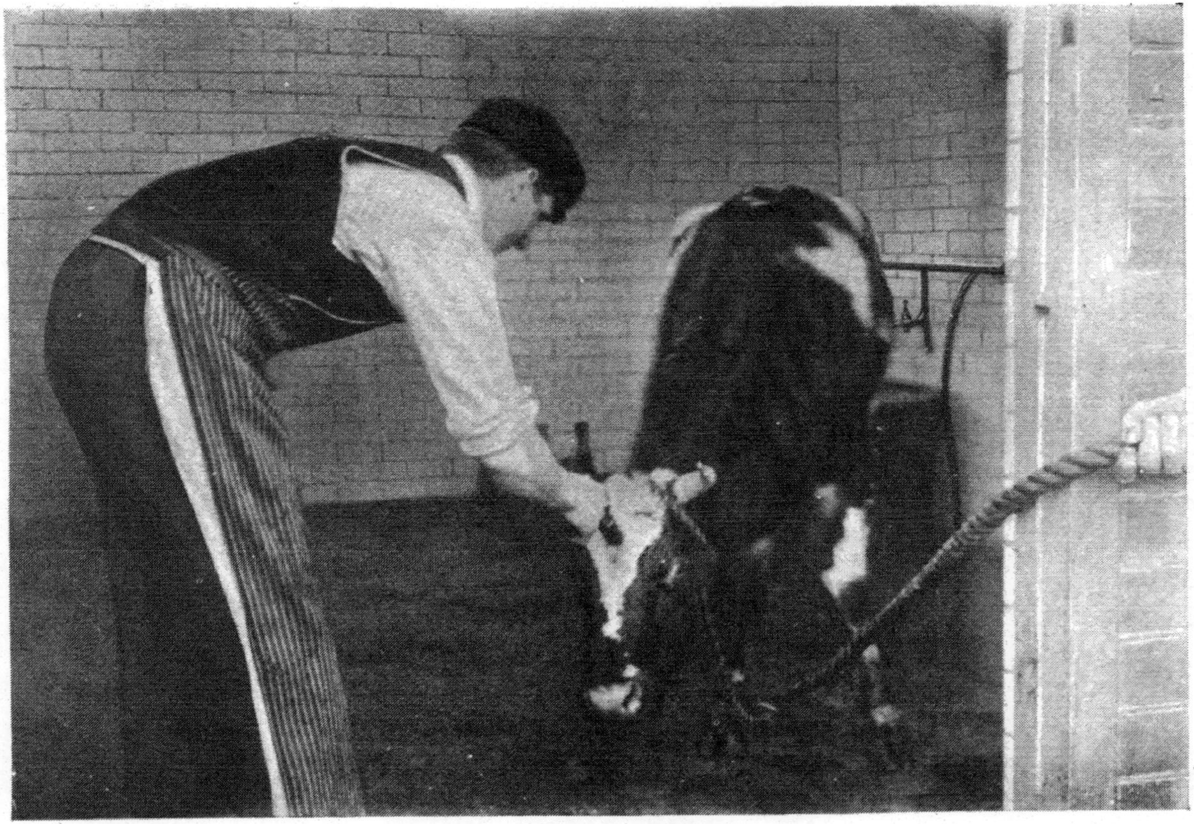

HUMANE SLAUGHTERING.

Behr pistol used for slaughtering large cattle.

an earnest believer, and on this ground, at any rate, some defence for it may be offered. This view of the matter is exactly expressed in an able letter which appeared in the *Spectator* shortly after the Admiralty Committee's report was issued, and which concludes with the following words:

'The Committee condemns, and, as I think, rightly condemns, the Jewish method of slaughtering oxen; but as long as the English people fail to insist that their smaller animals shall be killed as humanely as possible they are not justified in criticising others. The Jewish authorities, moreover, have carefully investigated the subject, and whilst keeping within the limits of a ritual which they hold to be essential, take certain precautions to avoid additional suffering. *We* kill callously for no better reason than that it is the custom of the trade, and in the name of common humanity it behoves us to set our own house in order without a moment's delay.'

Knocking Cattle.

CHAPTER IV

THE BUTCHER AND THE ABATTOIR

The evidence contained in the foregoing chapters is sufficient to prove that our slaughter-house system is in need of reform, and the reform which is indicated as the most obvious and the best consists in replacing the private slaughter-house by the public abattoir.

Instead of makeshift and insanitary structures stowed away in the courts and alleys of our great towns, we have in the abattoir a building expressly designed for the purpose for which it is intended, properly placed in an isolated position, and planned throughout in every detail —flooring, walls, drainage, ventilation and water-supply —with a view to cleanliness and sanitation.

All slaughtering operations being centralised in this building, the work of meat inspection becomes simple and effective, for, instead of having to scour over a whole town and pry into multitudinous private slaughter-houses, the meat inspector has merely to examine the carcasses of animals killed upon the premises.

Cruelty is prevented by the supervision of the abattoir officials, whose presence acts as a check on brutality, which would otherwise be undetected; and the best humane slaughtering appliances can be provided at small expense in an abattoir where the same apparatus can do duty for a number of different animals.

LEEDS ABATTOIR

The advantages—hygienic and humanitarian—of the public slaughter-house, which we have briefly stated, may carry weight with the general public, but they do not appeal to the butcher. The butcher dislikes the abattoir for various reasons. On his own premises he is his own master, and is free from supervision and control; in the abattoir he must submit to certain regulations, and does his work under the surveillance of the abattoir superintendent. With the system of public slaughter, moreover, his business is no longer private, for his fellow-butchers know exactly what class of animal he purchases. Besides this, there is the feeling of dislike to change of any kind. 'Butchers have always slaughtered on their own premises: why should they not continue to do so?' Finally, it is much more convenient for the butcher to have his slaughtering done close to his shop.

These are, we believe, the real reasons for the butcher's dislike to the abattoir. Such reasons are natural, and we can fully understand and appreciate them, though we do not feel that they should weigh for one moment against the vitally important advantages of the public slaughter-house system.

But let us consider another charge brought against the abattoir system. We are told that it is injurious to British agriculture. The butchers practically say, 'Do not trouble about us, but spare, oh, spare the farmer!' At first sight it is not very obvious why abattoirs should injure farmers, but the following is the alleged reason.

It is asserted that meat killed at an abattoir loses its freshness in transit to the butcher's shop, and that therefore home-grown meat does not command the price it otherwise would.

This fact is supposed to explain the falling-off in the

demand for home-grown meat, and to furnish an unanswerable argument against the public slaughter-house system. We should like to deal with this charge at some length, because it is intended to discredit the abattoir system with the British farmer, and with that large class who sympathise with the farmer in his hard struggle to make his industry pay.

And, firstly, I should like to ask, Why is it, if the abattoir is so fatal to the farmer, that in Denmark and Germany—countries where the abattoir system is fully established—agriculture is perhaps in as flourishing a state as here? The answer is, of course, obvious. It is not the abattoir, but the competition of the foreign meat trade, which is injuring the British farmer. The reason why the cattle-pens at Islington Market stand empty is because of the huge and ever-increasing imports of foreign meat and the enormous quantities of dead meat, also an increasing quantity, consigned for sale to Smithfield Market. The amount of fresh beef imported in 1906 from the United States alone reached the gigantic total of 2,426,644 cwts., and was more than double the value of what was sent here in 1890. Besides this, live cattle to the number of 398,887 were consigned to the United Kingdom (in 1906), and sheep to the number of 84,184. And this is only one item in our foreign meat bill. We have also to take into account the fresh beef sent from Argentina, the enormous consignments of mutton and 'Canterbury' lamb from Australia and New Zealand, the bacon from Denmark and Canada, etc.

At first the prejudice against foreign meat, especially prevalent among the lower classes, prevented the British farmer from experiencing the full effect of foreign meat competition, but that prejudice is fast disappearing, and the natural consequence has been a decline in the demand for the more expensive home-grown meat. To attempt, however, to explain this decline by the very partial introduction of the abattoir system into this country is absurd. We have decided for the policy of the 'large joint,' and the English farmer is paying the price.

We should wish here to refer to a special grievance which the British farmer has in connection with the foreign meat trade, and which consists in the absence of any mark by which foreign meat may be distinguished from home-grown. So long as foreign meat may be exposed for sale side by side with home-grown meat with no distinguishing mark to identify it, so long will the British farmer suffer from unfair competition.*

The obvious remedy for such a state of things might seem to be to have all foreign meat marked so as to be easily identified, but there are objections to this plan. The general public is averse to it. The purchaser of foreign meat is not always anxious to blazon the fact that he is buying a cheap article from motives of economy, and is quite satisfied that his joint should not be branded as 'foreign stuff.' But if there are objections to marking foreign meat, what of the alternative? Why should not home-grown meat be stamped? And here

* This is especially the case with what is called 'port-killed' meat—*i.e.*, the meat of foreign cattle shipped to a British port and slaughtered there. This point is well illustrated by the recent deputation of the Lincolnshire Farmers' Union to Earl Carrington. The deputation protested against the substitution of the term 'home-killed' for 'home-grown' in the wording of army meat contracts. Of course, the change in the specification makes it possible for the army contractor to supply 'port-killed' foreign meat instead of 'home-grown' to the detriment of the British farmer. Lord Carrington's answer to the deputation was that it was impossible for even an expert to distinguish 'home-bred' from 'home-killed' meat, and that the certificates given by the contractors vouching for their meat being 'home-grown' 'were not worth the paper they were written on'! If 'home-grown' cattle were killed at abattoirs and the meat officially stamped, such an answer could not have been given.

we touch the abattoir question again. If all home-grown cattle were slaughtered in public slaughter-houses, and every joint officially stamped, as is done in Germany, the public would have a guarantee, firstly, that the meat was genuine home-grown; secondly, that it had been officially inspected and found to be sound and wholesome; and thirdly, that it had been prepared under the superior sanitary conditions which prevail in a public as compared with a private slaughter-house.

In a very able article on abattoirs by A. E. Brindley, M.D., Medical Officer for Bury, Lancashire, which appeared in *Public Health* last April, the very pertinent remark is made that 'one of the greatest obstacles to abattoirs affording the full benefit to the public which they might, consists in the absence of any marking to indicate the fact that the meat has been killed in the abattoir and duly inspected.' If the official stamping of abattoir-killed meat were introduced, we should hear no more talk of such meat being of less value to the butcher as resembling foreign. It would be known at once as the best class of meat obtainable, and as such it would command the highest price.

Why people are so ready to patronise the foreign meat shop is because they cannot tell whether, when they pay for home-grown meat, they may not be served with foreign. If official stamping of home-grown meat were introduced, the farmer would look on the abattoir as his best friend.

But to return to the question of meat being spoiled in appearance by its journey from the abattoir to the shop. If there is any objection to carcasses being packed on one another in carts, why cannot the German plan be adopted, and vans be used in which the carcasses are hung from the roof, exactly as they would be in the shop? Surely, if the future of British agriculture is at stake it would be worth while to adopt this simple contrivance. As a matter of fact, I am somewhat sceptical of the ability of the average purchaser to at once distinguish by its exquisite appearance meat prepared in some squalid private slaughter-house from that which has been killed in the clean and airy slaughtering-hall of a first-class abattoir.

If the general public could view the unappetising interior of many a private slaughter-house, they would be more concerned about the sanitary conditions under which their meat is prepared than influenced by æsthetic considerations as to its appearance.

Again, if it is so essential that meat should be handled as little as possible, so that it may retain its bloom, where is this condition so completely fulfilled as in the abattoir? There we have mechanical appliances—the hoist, the overhead track, the travelling-hooks, by means of which a carcass is lifted and carried from the slaughtering-hall to the hanging-house, and from thence to the cold store, and automatically weighed without a finger being laid upon it.

And what of the meat sold by butchers—and there are many such—who have no slaughter-house of their own, who have to do their slaughtering on another butcher's premises, or who share a slaughter-house conjointly with other butchers? Do not they have to cart their meat from where it is killed to where it is sold, exactly as they would do if they were using an abattoir, the only difference being that, whereas under the present system they have to consult the convenience of other butchers, under the abattoir system they would have unrestricted slaughtering accommodation and every facility for their work? And the case is the same with meat salesmen who buy from the carcass butcher, but we hear no outcry about their meat being spoiled in transit.

We shall return later to this question of butchers who have to depend on other butchers for their slaughtering accommodation, and to whom an abattoir would be a convenience.

We have incidentally mentioned the cold store of the abattoir. What an inestimable boon this is to the butcher is obvious. In hot and trying weather a butcher may easily lose whole carcasses at a time, and thousands of pounds' worth of meat are thus wasted every year. In the private slaughter-houses there are seldom facilities for cooling meat, while in the abattoirs one of the main features is the cold storage, which enables the meat purveyor to chill down his carcasses to a keeping temperature after the animal heat has dissipated.

Again, take the butcher's standing grievance—the loss incurred by the purchase of an animal apparently healthy, which, when slaughtered, proves to be suffering from tuberculosis. Under the abattoir system, as found in Saxony and other parts of Germany, nothing of this kind can occur, for every animal must be insured before it is slaughtered, and if the carcass is confiscated the loss is covered by the insurance. Let us hear what Sir Richard Thorne has to say on the subject:

'How is the very proper demand for the butchers for uniformity in the conditions regulating the seizure of carcasses on account of tuberculosis to be met? How is such skilful handling of slightly tuberculous carcasses to be attained as will secure the removal of the diseased portions in such a way that no risk shall attach to the remainder? I only know one answer—namely, by the abolition, as far as practicable, of private slaughter-houses, by the provision in all large centres of population, whether technically styled urban or rural, of public slaughter-houses, under the direct control of the sanitary authorities and their officers, and by the adoption of measures which will, as soon as practicable, provide a class of skilled meat inspectors.

'The properly administered public slaughter-house is demanded as an act of justice to those trading in meat; it is demanded in the interests of public health and decency; it is demanded for the prevention of cruelty to the lower animals; and it is demanded in order to bring England, if not the United Kingdom, somewhat nearer to the level of other civilised nations in this matter.

'Public slaughter-houses, officered by skilled inspectors and supervised by medical officers of health, are urgently required, amongst other reasons, for the prevention of tuberculosis.'

Another point, and one which has not been sufficiently recognised in estimating the value of the abattoir system, is the facilities it offers for utilisation of so-called slaughter-house refuse.

One of the characteristics of the present age is the way in which 'waste' matter is converted into marketable produce. Under the private slaughter-house system blood and offal are simply got rid of with the least possible trouble as unremunerative waste. And as long as slaughtering is carried on piece-meal in small and scattered buildings this will always be the case. But if the work is centralised in one building, the blood and offal can be dealt with collectively, and converted by proper treatment into valuable material.

In Germany this has been done most effectively, and the revenue derived from dried blood and bone-meal helps considerably towards making the abattoir a financial success.

Finally, we come to the argument which up to now has told most potently against the adoption of the abattoir system—the argument of expense. A municipality may recognise the merits of the system, and may propose to build a public slaughter-house. But doubt as to the financial success of the undertaking often prevents action being taken in the matter. Especially at the present day, when so many of our towns have contracted heavy liabilities, they shrink from further commitments. 'An abattoir would be very good, but can we afford it, and will it pay its way?'

Why this question should be always asked in the case of abattoirs, the object of which is hygienic, when it is not asked in the case of other institutions with a similar object we do not know. Do sewage systems pay, or does sanitary inspection pay, or do hospitals pay? Why not do away with our expensive drainage arrangements, our sanitary inspection and our hospitals? None of them pay.

But to return. It may be confidently asserted that an abattoir will pay on one condition—namely, that all the butchers in a town use it; but, like any other institution, if it is not patronised it will not pay. Abattoirs are a financial success on the Continent. Where they are in the hands of companies they pay good dividends, and when owned by the municipality they help to reduce the rates.

As an attempt has been recently made to urge the large sums spent on abattoirs in Germany as an argument against introducing the public slaughter-house system into this country, we should like to say a few words on this subject.

We are told that we cannot build abattoirs at a less charge than 15s. per head of the population, this being the cost of some that have been built in Germany. We venture to say that the case of Germany is by no means analogous, and that no arguments can be drawn from the cost of German abattoirs for several reasons.

SOUTH SHIELDS ABATTOIR.

ENTRANCE.

SLAUGHTERING-HALL.

Opened October 24, 1906. The lairage accommodates 700 sheep and 100 cattle. The cooling-room will contain carcasses of 500 beasts, sheep and other cattle. Piggeries, with eighteen covered lairs and open standage for 300 pigs. Total cost, including site, £17,500. Population of South Shields, 90,000. Cost per head, less than 4s.

Firstly, because in Germany the vast majority of meat is home-bred, and foreign meat is excluded. A far larger abattoir is therefore required in a German town, where the meat is all killed on the spot, than in one of the same size in England, where a large proportion of the inhabitants buy foreign meat.* Secondly, a German abattoir often includes a great deal more than we think necessary or desirable for abattoirs here. In a German abattoir, beside the slaughter-house proper and the cold store, we find an ice-making plant, a sausage factory, a *Freibank* or certified cooked-meat shop, a laboratory, a pickling room, even sometimes a soup-kitchen, a dogs' home, a restaurant, and a public swimming-bath. Again, German abattoirs are often constructed with costly materials and an amount of ornamentation which are not absolutely essential. The slaughtering-hall at the Straubing abattoir, for instance, is faced with white marble.

Abattoirs, indeed, are often built in such decorative style that the public slaughter-house is not unfrequently the handsomest building in the town.

That in Germany, where public money is not, as a rule, recklessly squandered, it should be thought worth while to spend so lavishly on abattoirs is a matter which should give us food for reflection. Moreover, in spite of

* The following figures, showing the relative numbers of animals slaughtered in English and German towns of the same size, bear out the writer's contention as to the greater slaughtering accommodation needed in the latter :

	Population.	Beafts.	Calves.	Sheep.	Pigs.	Total.
Cassel ...	81,741	6,848	15,254	9,520	23,353	54,975
Karlsruhe ...	81,414	10,152	17,963	3,223	33,247	64,585
Augsburg ...	80,800	12,738	22,100	3,766	43,810	81,414

	Population.	Beasts and Calvse.	Sheep.	Pigs.	Total.
Coventry ...	83,900	8,424	17,628	8,476	34,528

the large original outlay, these institutions are financially successful.

Why is it, therefore, that in England abattoirs, generally speaking, barely pay their way? Simply because in England, though we have abattoirs, we have not the abattoir system—in other words, though a town may build an abattoir, it has no power when the abattoir is built to close the private slaughter-houses. 'Urban authorities in England and Wales may, if they think fit, provide slaughter-houses.' But no power is given to a sanitary authority to close private slaughter-houses on the erection of public slaughter-houses.

The effect of this admirable arrangement is, firstly, to perpetuate the very nuisance (of private slaughter-houses) which the abattoir has been built to abolish, and, secondly, to make the financial success of the abattoir almost impossible.

How, indeed, is it possible for an institution of this kind to pay its way when the butchers, whose slaughtering dues form its revenue, are allowed to continue to slaughter on their own premises?

That they will continue to do so as long as they are allowed to is obvious; for, beside the natural preference which they have for their own slaughter-houses, it is not likely that they will wish to contribute to the financial success of an institution which they dislike.

The only resource for the authorities is to make the slaughtering dues extremely low in the hope of getting butchers to use the abattoir, the result being that the revenue obtained is inadequate. Of course, this lowering of charges will not induce those who have their own slaughter-houses to close them and use the abattoir, but it will affect a class of butchers to whom we have already referred, who depend on other butchers for slaughtering accommodation, and who are already paying slaughtering dues in the form of rent for the use of other butchers' premises. These men find it quite as cheap to use the abattoir, and perhaps more convenient.

A very sound arrangement is adopted in Scotland, where the slaughtering dues are periodically adjusted. If it is found that they are too low to meet expenses, they are raised; if otherwise, they are lowered.

With the object of ascertaining to what extent abattoirs in this country are a financial success or otherwise, the writer recently addressed a circular letter of inquiry to the authorities of towns known to possess public slaughter-houses.

The circular contained the following questions in order:

1. Is your local abattoir a financial success—that is to say, are the receipts sufficient to cover working expenses, pay interest on original outlay, and furnish a sinking fund, however small?
2. If the abattoir does not pay its way, to what do you attribute the fact?
3. What number of private slaughter-houses are still in existence?
4. What is the scale of slaughtering dues?
5. Is any profit made by converting slaughter-house refuse into marketable produce?
6. Do you consider that the abattoir has justified its existence on sanitary and humanitarian grounds?

In all, forty-two replies were received, and the writer takes this opportunity of thanking those town clerks, medical officers, and other officials who replied to his inquiries, for their kindness and courtesy in so doing.

Of the forty-two replies to question 1, it was most satisfactory to find that seventeen, or something like 40 per cent., were in the affirmative. This is sufficient to prove that abattoirs can be made to pay even under

CATTLE MARKET, GLASGOW.

the very adverse conditions prevailing at the present time. And if an abattoir can be made to pay in one town, why should it not in another?

The following is a complete list of those abattoirs which comply with the conditions stated in question 1.

Hereford: Receipts, £207 4s. 7d.; expenditure, £132 14s. 11d.; balance, £74 9s. 8d.

Port Glasgow: Simply stated to be a financial success.

Newport, Monmouth: Average expenses, £451; receipts, £515.

Cardiff: Roath abattoir pays. No particulars.

Glasgow: Profit of £983.

Leicester: Financial success. No figures given. Forty private slaughter-houses still existing.

Halifax: 'Yes, practically so.'

Chorley, Lancashire: Balance, £23.

Manchester: Financial success. No balance-sheet issued.

Dundee: Surplus, £469 7s. 6d. Rents periodically adjusted.

Aberavon: Financial success.

Chesterfield: Financial success.

Blackburn: £110 was made from the abattoir last financial year.

Belfast: Makes about £800 per annum.

Edinburgh: Surplus revenue at the close of this year, £924 13s. 6d.

Lancaster: 'Yes; one year's receipts may be below amount and next year's above.'

Paisley: Financial success.

Of other towns from which answers were received, Blackpool, Douglas, Rotherham and Wolverhampton pay working expenses. In the case of Croydon and Huddersfield the loss is stated to be 'slight,' and in

LINCOLN ABATTOIR.

NEW SLAUGHTERING-HALL.

OLD SLAUGHTERING-HALL.

the case of Kendal, Middlesbrough, and Worcester the loss does not exceed £40.

But what is most instructive are the answers to question 2. We give several specimens. The reply from Cheltenham states: 'If all the butchers used the abattoir, it would pay its way easily. We have no power to compel the butchers to use the abattoir.'

ILFRACOMBE: 'To existence of private slaughter-houses which we cannot get rid of.'

BOLTON: 'On account of the large number of private slaughter-houses.'

KENDAL: 'Low charges to draw customers and secure soundness of people's food.'

PLYMOUTH: 'Too low charges.'

READING: 'The rents have always been too low.'

MIDDLESBROUGH: 'Butchers will crowd into small, badly-constructed, ill-ventilated private slaughter-houses, and suffer any inconvenience rather than kill in our public slaughter-house.'

LINCOLN: 'If all private slaughter-houses were closed, the abattoir might pay.'

WORCESTER: 'The existence of so many private slaughter-houses (thirty-three) is the real cause of comparative failure.'

We might quote many more answers of a similar tenor, but the above are sufficient to prove what we have already stated—namely, that what prevents abattoirs from paying is the coexistence of private slaughter-houses. To compete with these the abattoir has to cut prices, as is evident from the fact that the average charge in this country for slaughtering a beast is from 1s. to 1s. 6d.; calves, 3d. to 6d.; sheep, 1d. to 3d.; and pigs, 3d. to 9d. In Germany the slaughtering fee for beasts is from 5s. to 6s.; for pigs, 1s. 6d. to 3s.; for calves

GENERAL VIEW OF STOCK-YARDS, CHICAGO.

1s.; and for sheep, 6d.; so that the English butcher gets off cheaply in comparison. It is not surprising that our abattoirs find it difficult to make both ends meet.

To question 5 the answers were not very satisfactory, little, apparently, being done at present to utilise slaughter-house refuse. Sometimes it is sold to farmers as manure at a nominal price, or even given away to cover cost of the removal. There is no doubt that in this matter there is room for improvement. Dr. Brindley, of Bury, Lancashire, states that 'an advantage which has resulted from the establishment of an abattoir has been found in the disposal of offal. Certain portions which were formerly wasted in great part now find a ready sale—*e.g.*, the intestines of cattle fetch 1s. each, and those of sheep 1½d. each, thus almost paying the dues charged for slaughtering.'

At the present moment the name of Chicago is not a word to conjure with, but, however little we may admire some of the methods of the Chicago packers, the wonderful way in which they have utilised waste products may give us a hint as to what may be done in this direction.*

* The following quotation from the *Daily Mail* as bearing on this point may be of interest:

'The real founder of the American Beef Trust—the greatest food monopoly the world has yet seen—was Philip Danforth Armour. In his Chicago meat factory he first saw the possibilities of utilising on the spot the lost by-products and offal from slaughtered animals. . . . Of all the features of the industry, the by-products are the most interesting and the most amazing. If a steer weigh 1,500 pounds, it dresses out approximately at 800 pounds of beef. The remainder of the animal—hide, head, feet, blood, fats, casings—with the offal from the hogs and sheep, furnishes material for the by-product plants. The head and the feet go to the fertiliser and glue works; the horn is cut off to be converted into combs, buttons, hairpins, and fertiliser; the hard shin-bone is cut from the feet, and with the thigh and blade bones made into knife and tooth brush handles, pipe mouthpieces, buttons, and bone ornaments, and the waste into glue and fertiliser. The hoof is made into hair-pins, buttons, yellow prussiate, and fertiliser. The feet, knuckles, hide clippings, and small bones are made into glue, gelatin, isinglass, neat's-foot oil, tallow, grease, stearine, and fertiliser.

At the Edinburgh abattoir the proceeds of sale of blood, manure, hoofs, spurs, tallow, ox feet parings, and bones for the year ending May 15, 1906, amounted to £1,043 12s. 9d.

With regard to the sixth and last question, the evidence is practically unanimous in favour of the abattoir on sanitary and humanitarian grounds. The statement by the Medical Officer for Cheltenham is worth quoting :

'The best of the private slaughter-houses in the town is a wretched place, compared with the slaughter-house in the abattoir, in regard to light, ventilation, cleanliness, structure, conveniences, treatment of the animals, and general sanitary efficiency. Inspection of animals and meat is rendered possible, and the amount of diseased meat discovered and destroyed is ten times as much in the abattoir as in the private slaughter-houses, though most animals are killed in the latter.'

'The cattle tails go to the curled-hair works, and the bristles to the bristle works. The tallow and grease go to the soap works to be converted into toilet and laundry soaps, washing-powder, and all grades of glycerine. The pig's stomach and pancreas, and the sheep's thyroid and other glands, go to the pharmaceutical laboratory for pepsins, pancreatins, and desiccated thyroids. The blood and tankage and all waste of a nitrogenous or phosphatic character are made into fertilisers of different analyses and into stock and poultry foods. Phosphoric acid and phosphorus, bone-black and black pigments, sulphate of ammonia, bone oil, and many other things are also made from packing-house waste.'

CHAPTER V

THE ABATTOIR QUESTION A MATTER FOR LEGISLATION

THE obvious inference to be drawn from the evidence given in the preceding chapter is that the only reasonable arrangement consists in investing municipalities with the power to close private slaughter-houses, with due compensation and after proper notice has been given, when once an abattoir has been built.

This is what has been done in Germany with excellent results; nor need we look so far as the Continent, but only across the border, to see this very system in operation.

'In burghs in Scotland, by the Burgh Police Act, 1892, when the commissioners have provided a public slaughter-house, no other place within the burgh may be used for slaughtering. A similar result has been obtained in Edinburgh and Glasgow, where not a single private slaughter-house is permitted to exist.'*

Apparently, there is some idea that to compel a butcher to use an abattoir involves some hardship to him. As a matter of fact, as has been well said, there is no more hardship in compelling a butcher to slaughter at an abattoir instead of in a private slaughter-house than there would be in compelling a householder to join his

* Report of Royal Commission on Tuberculosis.

house-drains on to a main drainage system instead of using a noxious cesspool outside his back door. The householder very probably complains of hardship, and with as much justice as the butcher who is compelled to slaughter at an abattoir.

But I would go further, and assert that to many butchers not only is the using of the abattoir no hardship, but a positive boon. We have already referred to butchers who have no slaughter-house of their own, but who pay for the right of slaughtering on other butchers' premises. These men, as is shown by the following letter from a butcher in the writer's own town, would welcome the establishment of an abattoir.

'*To the "Meat Trade Journal."*

'SIR,

'Will you allow me a few lines in your valuable paper to ask if something cannot be done to help the poor little butchers in Coventry? Now, we have no public slaughter-houses, and I am led to understand that the Corporation will not build one; consequently poor little butchers like myself have to be under the thumb of the bigger butchers who have slaughter-houses, and call themselves "wholesale butchers." Now, at times it means a considerable loss to the likes of myself; for instance, I pay rent, and kill a beast and two sheep, but the wholesale man said: "You cannot kill your beast to-night, as my men have a lot of beasts to do for the wholesale trade. I will, however, sell you a side of beef and a sheep for Tuesday's trade." The consequence was I had to purchase a side of beef and one sheep at the rate of ½d. per pound more than the market price. I think there might be a public slaughter-house built near the live market, where there is plenty of land, or else grant licenses to those who have room at the back of their shops. I can speak of some slaughter-houses that are adjoining dwelling-houses, and there is nothing said about them. But there's myself and other butchers who have tried for a license and failed, because they say, "It's too near the houses." I cannot see how that can be detrimental, because we have good inspectors here; and if a private slaughter-house is kept as it should be, it is sweeter and cleaner than lots of the dwelling-houses. I hope some of my fellow-traders will take this matter up and corroborate my views.'

Whatever we may think of the writer's plea for more private slaughter-houses, we cannot but sympathise with him in his demand for more slaughtering accommodation. His is a real grievance, and the attitude of those butchers who, having private slaughter-houses of their own, oppose the building of an abattoir, which would supply accommodation for other butchers, is a very selfish one.

At the present moment there are in Coventry seventy-nine butchers and fifty-two slaughter-houses; there are, therefore, twenty-seven butchers without separate accommodation who have to slaughter as best they can on other butchers' premises. Such a state of things is neither fair to the butcher nor to the British farmer from whom the butcher buys. What is wanted is unrestricted slaughtering accommodation under sanitary conditions, so that every encouragement may be given to butchers to buy and kill home-grown meat.

The state of things in Coventry is not exceptional, and, as in other towns where some attempt has been made to reform the slaughter-house system, the position is an illogical one. For either an abattoir is built and the private slaughter-houses are not closed, in which case the abattoir is a financial failure, or the slaughter-houses are partially closed and no abattoir built, in which case the butchers are driven to become purveyors of foreign meat, to the detriment of the British farmer.

The closing of slaughter-houses by refusing to renew licenses has up till now done but little good, and merely causes irritation and discontent; for it does not put an end to the evil system, while those who are dispossessed of their slaughter-houses feel themselves aggrieved. The question, too, is further complicated by the distinction between licensed and registered slaughter-houses.

'While a licensed slaughter-house can be closed permanently after two convictions of the occupier for non-compliance with the by-laws, or for having sold unsound or diseased meat on the premises, the same does not apply to registered slaughter-houses, the latter term including all those which were already in existence at the time of the application to the town or district of the Towns Improvement Clauses Act, 1847. In respect to these, a closing order cannot be obtained unless two convictions are obtained against the owner or proprietor; and, inasmuch as the owner or proprietor is hardly ever the occupier also, it follows that, however many convictions may be obtained against the occupier, there is no power of closing the slaughter-house.'

In Brighton, for instance, all the twenty-five slaughter-houses are registered, and in no case is the owner or proprietor at the same time the occupier.

The fact is that the whole slaughter-house question requires to be dealt with broadly, and to be made the subject of legislation which would by a few simple enactments sweep away the muddled complexity of local regulations which at present impede all reform.

In spite of the great advance in sanitary knowledge which has taken place in recent years, the last great enactment relating to public health—so far as the whole of England, excluding London, is concerned—is the Public Health Act of 1875. During the thirty years which have since elapsed some minor and amending Acts have been passed. The usual history of the growth of an amending Act is that some local authority, more enterprising than its fellows, and probably more foreseeing, applies for special powers in regard to some sanitary matters in a local Act; if successful in carrying these powers through the various Parliamentary Committees, other authorities, in an imitative way, if they think that these powers might be of use to them, introduce them in their local Acts if a time comes when they are for some purpose or other endeavouring to get a local Act through Parliament. The precedent having been once established, the imitating authorities find their thorny way through Parliament considerably smoother. If the powers obtained accidentally receive sufficient attention and support, there is a chance of a Bill being introduced applying to the whole country, giving these powers to all local authorities; in some cases they are applied compulsorily, while in others they are adoptive. The result of this method of evolution is in the highest degree confusing. We not only have sanitary laws quite distinct in England, Scotland and Ireland, but we have separate, though in many respects similar, ones in London, while, further, there are multitudinous sanitary authorities throughout the country. We thus have quite different methods of dealing, say, with insanitary property in one town to those existing in a neighbouring town close by: the powers possessed by different local authorities in the matter of abolishing private slaughter-houses and substituting abattoirs might almost be described as the colours of the rainbow.

The excuse, if any exists, for this state of things is that of different local circumstances; yet we live in a small island. Nature has not found it necessary to endow us with any great variety as far as our anatomy is concerned: the physiological laws which govern the functions of our various organs appear to be very much the same whether we live in the Orkneys or at Hampstead. Insanitary conditions are of equal importance wherever met with. Diseased meat is equally obnoxious whether in town or country. It may be suggested with some show of reason that the ogre of 'local circumstances' should not be allowed to bulk so largely in our sanitary legislation.

In conclusion, may we suggest that, should our slaughter-house system be made a subject for legislation, that legislation could proceed on no sounder lines than the recommendations of the Royal Commission on Tuberculosis in 1898, which we herewith append:

'1. We recommend that in all towns and municipal boroughs in England and Wales, and in Ireland, powers be conferred on the authorities similar to those conferred on Scottish corporations and municipalities by the Burgh Police (Scotland) Act, 1892, viz.:

'(*a*) When the local authority in any town or urban district in England and Wales and Ireland have provided a public slaughter-house, power be conferred on them to declare that no other place within the town or borough shall be used for slaughtering, except that a period of three years be allowed to the owners of existing registered private slaughter-houses to apply their premises to other purposes. The term of three years to date, in those places where adequate public slaughter-houses exist, from the public announcement by the local authority that the use of such public slaughter-houses is obligatory, or, in those places where public slaughter-houses have not been erected, from the public announcement by the local authority that tenders for their erection have been accepted.

'(*b*) That local authorities be empowered to require all meat slaughtered elsewhere than in a public slaughter-house, and brought into the district for sale, to be taken to a place or places where such meat may be inspected; and that local authorities be empowered to make a charge to cover the reasonable expenses attendant on such inspection.

'(*c*) That when a public slaughter-house has been established, inspectors shall be engaged to inspect all animals immediately after slaughter, and *stamp* the joints of all carcasses passed as sound.'

To these recommendations might we add that of the Admiralty Committee on Humane Slaughtering: that every animal slaughtered be stunned or otherwise rendered unconscious before blood is drawn.*

* Since the above was written the second interim report by the Commission appointed in 1901 to inquire into the relation between human and bovine tuberculosis has appeared.

This report states, as beyond all doubt, that human and bovine tuberculosis are identical—a point which had hitherto been in dispute.

We need not insist on the enormous importance of this discovery, or the additional argument it furnishes for the introduction of the only possible system under which meat inspection can be efficient, namely, the public slaughter-house system.

APPENDIX

STATEMENTS BY MEDICAL OFFICERS WITH REGARD TO PRIVATE SLAUGHTER-HOUSES AND ABATTOIRS.

BLACKBURN.

PUBLIC abattoirs are, in my opinion, infinitely preferable to private slaughter-houses. I am strongly in favour of the abolition of all private slaughter-houses and the erection of public abattoirs instead. In Blackburn we have both systems at work, and I can unhesitatingly say that public abattoirs are infinitely preferable, owing to their superior sanitation, greater facilities for efficient inspection, and concentration of work.

ALFRED GREENWOOD.

BIRKENHEAD.

There can be no satisfactory or efficient inspection except in towns with public abattoirs. Private slaughter-houses are very frequently misused, and help the distribution of slink meat. This is my own experience. I consider that every private slaughter-house should be abolished in large towns. I have never heard of any town reverting from the public to the private slaughter-house system.

R. SIDNEY MARSDEN.

BERMONDSEY.

That all slaughtering should be done in public abattoirs under proper supervision.

R. K. BROWN.

BURNLEY.

Public abattoirs by all means. You can then inspect all slaughtered meat. The public have confidence in the meat they eat.

THOMAS DEAN.

BRIGHTON.

There is no doubt that the latter (private slaughter-houses) in large towns are a serious cause of nuisance and danger to health. There can be no such thorough inspection of meat with this system as with public abattoirs.

A. NEWSHOLME.

BRADFORD.

It is absolutely necessary to have public abattoirs for the efficient inspection of meat.

W. ARNOLD EVANS.

BETHNAL GREEN.

I think private slaughter-houses in large towns should be abolished.

G. T. BATE, M.D.

BURY.

Abattoirs, combined with cold-air stores, may be advantageous to both Sanitary Authority and trade, due regard being paid to (*a*) situation, (*b*) economical construction. I am in favour of branch slaughter-houses (one or more) in large towns.

A. E. BRINDLEY.

BIRMINGHAM.

I have not the slightest hesitation in saying that inspection of dead meat for human food cannot be efficient unless public abattoirs be established by the municipality, or by the butchers themselves.

JOHN ROBERTSON.

BATTERSEA.

The public slaughter-house is an essential part of any really efficient system of meat inspection. For the protection of the public health private slaughter-houses should be abolished, and all slaughtering carried out in public slaughter-houses under the direct supervision and control of the responsible officers of the Sanitary Authority.

G. F. McCLEARY.

BRISTOL.

I consider that public abattoirs are a necessity for the due and proper supervision of the meat-supplies of large towns, and that England should follow the Continental lead in the establishment of an effective system, leading to full control of the meat-supply.

D. S. DAVIES, M.D.

CHELTENHAM.

There can be no question in any sane person's mind that it is to the public advantage for all animals intended for food to be slaughtered in a public abattoir, where the animals and meat can be inspected, and the sale of diseased and unsound prevented.

J. H. GARRATT.

CARDIFF.

Impossible to carry out meat-inspection without public abattoir.

EDWARD WALFORD.

DERBY.

I have reported in favour of a municipal abattoir.

W. J. HOWARTH.

DEPTFORD.

In favour of public abattoirs.

H. W. ROBERTS.

FINSBURY.

Public abattoirs much preferable wherever practicable.

GEORGE NEWMAN, M.D.

GREENWICH.

My own opinion is distinctly in favour of a public abattoir, as opposed to a private slaughter-house; and in the course of my inspection of the private slaughter-houses I find often they are not in use because the butchers make use of the public abattoir, although this is situated at some considerable distance.

E. G. ANNIS.

GRIMSBY.

From a public health point of view abattoirs are undoubtedly the best.

T. NEWBY, M.D.

HAMPSTEAD.

Am clearly of opinion that in the interests of public health, private slaughter-houses should be abolished where practicable, and public abattoirs provided.

HERBERT LITTLEJOHN.

HUDDERSFIELD.

Private slaughter-houses are objectionable from more than one point of view. Not only is it advisable for the avoidance of ordinary nuisances that private slaughter-houses should be done away with so far as possible, but also because it is in such places that the trade in diseased and slink meat finds a home. That private slaughter-houses constituted nuisances, and required supervision and control, is evidenced by the fact that in some places, long before the passing of the ordinary laws, special regulations were in force with regard to them.

S. G. MOORE.

HALIFAX.

I advocate public abattoirs, because it is impossible to inspect meat efficiently in private slaughter-houses. It has a tendency to cause a better class of meat to be bought, because one butcher does not like it to be seen that another has better meat than himself. Also the Corporation has control, and can see that no nuisance is created.

JAS. T. NEECH.

HACKNEY.

I am of the opinion that public abattoirs are preferable to private slaughter-houses.

J. KING WARRY, M.D.

ISLINGTON.

They are an absolute necessity for the prevention of the sale of diseased or unsound meat.

A. E. HARRIS.

KENSINGTON.

In favour of public slaughter-houses, which I have advocated for more than thirty years.

T. ORME DUDFIELD.

KINGSTON-UPON-HULL.

From a public health and administrative point of view, a public abattoir would be a decided improvement on private slaughter houses, and should, in my opinion, be established in all large towns.

J. WRIGHT MASON.

LEICESTER.

I think it would be better if all private slaughter-houses could be abolished

C. K. MILLARD.

LEEDS.

Public abattoirs alone ought to be permitted in large towns.

J. SPOTTISWOODE CAMERON.

LEYTON, ESSEX.

I am strongly in favour of public abattoirs.

A. F. PESKETT.

LONDON (COUNTY).

I do not think that any proper system of meat inspection can be established so long as animals are killed in private slaughter-houses.

SHIRLEY F. MURPHY.

MANCHESTER.

Private slaughter-houses should, in my opinion, be replaced by a public abattoir or abattoirs.

JAMES NIVEN.

NORTHAMPTON.

Public abattoirs much to be preferred.

JAMES BEATTY.

NORWICH.

In favour of public abattoirs unquestionably.

H. COOPER PATTIN, M.D.

PRESTON.

I am satisfied that for killing the animals in a cleanly, humane, and satisfactory manner, and for the proper inspection of meat, a public abattoir is infinitely superior to private slaughter-houses.

F. O. PILKINGTON.

December 12, 1905.

Year by year I am confirmed in the above opinion; and gradually, since the erection of the abattoir, the butchers of the town have come to see its advantages, and have made greater use of it.

H. O. P.

PLYMOUTH.

Far superior in every way.

F. M. WILLIAMS.

PADDINGTON.

Public abattoirs in every way the more desirable.

REGINALD DUDFIELD.

SALFORD.

Public abattoirs are decidedly to be preferred, as inspection in private slaughter-houses cannot possibly be satisfactory unless an unduly large staff is maintained.

C. H. TATTERSALL.

SOUTHWARK.

Personally, I have reported strongly on the advantage arising from the provision of public abattoirs, and I believe the same opinion is held by the medical officers of other boroughs. One of the chief points in regard to private slaughter-houses is the facility it gives the owners for disposing of carcasses that would hardly pass the inspection at Smithfield Market.

E. H. MILLSON.

ST. HELENS.

Personally, I am strongly in favour of them, as their existence ensures the only really effectual inspection of meat.

F. DREW HARRIS.

SWANSEA.

Public incomparably better.

EVAN DAVIES.

STOCKPORT.

Public slaughter-houses are infinitely to be preferred, so far as the safety of the public health is concerned. It is next to impossible to keep an adequate watch on private slaughter-houses. I have known many butchers who have tried public slaughter-houses, and though they have had private ones of their own, they have discontinued the use of the private ones voluntarily.

MEREDITH YOUNG, M.D.

SHEFFIELD.

I am strongly in favour of public abattoirs.

HAROLD SCURFIELD
(As Medical Officer of Health of Sunderland).

ST. MARYLEBONE.

Public abattoirs are preferable.

A. WINTER BLYTH.

SOUTHPORT.

For purposes of meat inspection there can be no difference of opinion as to the superiority of public slaughter-houses over private ones; in fact, it is practically quite impossible to get satisfactory meat inspection except in public slaughter-houses.

JOHN J. WEAVER.

STOKE NEWINGTON.

In my opinion public abattoirs are superior to private slaughter-houses, from whatever standpoint the subject is considered.

HENRY KENWOOD.

TOTTENHAM.

My own opinion, based on practical experience in various countries for many years, is strongly in favour of public abattoirs, as the only efficient means of safeguarding the public against ignorant and unconscientious butchers.

J. F. BUTLER-HOGAN, B.A., M.D.

WIGAN.

My strong opinion is that public abattoirs should be established, and I don't believe any Corporation will revert to re-licensing of private slaughter-houses, as the majority are totally unfit for the purpose.

WILLIAM BERRY.

WOOLWICH.

That England, and especially London, is very much behind the Continent. Where public abattoirs are the rule, meat inspection is efficient, and the public benefited both in security from disease and pecunarily by the profit of the slaughter-houses. I have personally found this so at Cologne.

SIDNEY DAVIES.

WALTHAMSTOW.

In favour of public abattoirs, as being more easily supervised, and consequently more efficient.

J. J. CLARKE.

West Ham.

Public abattoirs distinctly advantageous for convenience of inspection.

CHARLES SANDERS.

Wolverhampton.

Private slaughter-houses objectionable—partly because they are apt to be a nuisance, but mainly because of the hindrance they offer to efficient inspection of meat. Am strongly in favour of public abattoirs.

HENRY MALET.

Wandsworth.

In favour of public abattoirs.

CALDWELL SMITH, M.D.

PART II

THE GERMAN ABATTOIR*

BY

HERR HUGO HEISS,

ABATTOIR DIRECTOR OF STRAUBING, BAVARIA, AND AUTHOR OF A PRIZE ESSAY ON HUMANE SLAUGHTERING

CHAPTER I

A RETROSPECT

THERE was a time in Germany—a time that dates as far back as the thirteenth century—when guilds and corporations flourished in the land. In those days all handicraftsmen were united in various fraternities—unconscious prototypes of the trading companies of to-day. Of these fraternities the butchers, even in those early days, built themselves premises for the joint use of all members of their guild. The object with which these public slaughter-houses were built was not the sanitary improvement of the towns. Far from it—commercial advantage was the sole motive for their erection.

If we glance through historical records bearing on the meat-supply of our towns in the Middle Ages, we find that in the year 1276 a decree of the city of Augsburg commanded that all horned cattle brought within the walls should be slaughtered in the public slaughter-house. In the records of the towns of Regensburg and

* *Vide* preface.

Hamburg we find similar ordinances, and in the latter town the municipal slaughter-house was in use from the middle of the thirteenth to the nineteenth century. In Hamburg, too, we find the municipal authorities giving permission for the carcasses of slaughtered animals to be exposed to view in order to attract purchasers and ensure a speedy sale.

Cologne had a public slaughter-house in 1370, and in the case of Nordhausen, in Thuringia, we notice the first instance of a decree enjoining the use of the public slaughter-house, not only for all slaughtering operations, but also for the manufacture of sausages.

In Nuremburg a public slaughter-house was first built in 1349 and restored in 1530. It continued to be used till 1891, when the new abattoir and cattle market, an establishment on the very latest lines, was opened.

According to a municipal ordinance of the year 1348, the butchers of the town of Chemnitz were forbidden to slaughter 'in the public streets' or 'in front of houses,' and were ordered to perform all slaughtering in the public slaughter-house.

This example was followed by the town of Aix-la-Chapelle in 1558, and Gera had its own slaughter-house in 1658.

A public slaughter-house was built in Berlin in 1661, altered in 1725, and used till 1810.

It would be tedious to quote the names of the various towns which have possessed public slaughter-houses from the Middle Ages to the beginning of the last century. We only wish to draw attention to the fact that institutions of the kind existed in German towns from the earliest times, and that, moreover, the towns made their use compulsory.

The attempt on the part of municipalities to improve

our slaughter-house system dates, therefore, from several hundred years ago.

The long and exhausting wars through which Germany passed (with the natural consequence that much territory changed hands) were not without a certain influence on the establishment of slaughter-houses.

The decline of the guilds also contributed to the decay and neglect of existing institutions, and the beginning of the nineteenth century saw a state of social stagnation prevailing. It was Napoleon who, at the beginning of the nineteenth century, ordered public slaughter-houses to be built in the towns of States which he had just subjected. His object, however, was probably not so much improved sanitation, as the regular supply of meat for his troops. Even at the present day we come across slaughtering premises which owe their origin to buildings constructed at that time.

It was not until the end of the 'War of Liberation' that fresh and vigorous life seemed to infuse itself into Germany, and that more prosperous times promised further development of the public slaughter-house system. Many years had, indeed, to elapse before establishments of this kind were erected which deserve to be regarded as an example for imitation, or which were worthy of the times in which we live.

At length, however, it was felt that the time had come to break with the intolerable state of things which had gradually grown up—a state of things which has its counterpart in England at the present day.

It would be a mistake to suppose that, at the time we speak of, slaughter-houses, even of the most modest description, were to be found in all German towns. We cannot even boast that things were any better in Germany at that time than they are nowadays in England.

Let us picture to ourselves a typical German slaughter-house of that date, and some are even now to be found in remote country districts.

A gloomy-looking hovel, with dilapidated roof and broken window-panes, the flooring out of repair and pitted with holes in which blood and water stand in pools. Walls splashed with blood, cobwebs hanging in every corner. In the whole building a vague, indescribable smell of blood, dirt, and manure. No proper water-pipes, but a defective well supplies all water used for cleansing purposes. For hoisting up the carcasses dirty ropes hang from the beams of the roof, to which are attached gambrels of primitive make, clumsily raised by windlasses worked with bars.

The animal to be slaughtered, worried by barking dogs, is forced into the slaughter-house, and, when its head has been tightly bound to a gambrel, the slaughter-man attempts to stun it with his axe. Sometimes he is at once successful, sometimes repeated blows, causing intense pain, are needed before the animal, groaning and bellowing with pain, sinks to the ground mortally wounded. The arteries of the throat are then opened and the blood collected. At length life is extinct and the slaughter-man can proceed to skin his beast. The intestines are then removed, placed, perhaps, on an old door or dirty boards, and carried to the neighbouring river.

The contents of the intestines are emptied into the stream, and the intestines themselves *cleaned* with the dirty river-water into which some evil-smelling drain discharges itself close by.

The carcass is left hanging in the foul and tainted building, and is taken down when cold on the following day. There is many a trace to show that rats, cats, and dogs, which regularly seek a living in such places, have helped themselves to their share.

Often, too, we notice that buildings of this kind are

polluted with human excrement. Later on the meat is removed to the butcher's shop in carts of questionable cleanliness, with no covering over it. There it remains hanging till it is sold in spite of the appearance it acquires by the continued process of decomposition. Or, again, it may be laid on ice in dirty ice-cellars, where it becomes coated with a greasy mould and contracts a decidedly 'mousy' smell, which cannot be removed even by washing. Meat laid on ice, moreover, always has an unpleasantly red colour.

In the times we are speaking of any place was thought suitable for slaughtering small cattle in—a wash-house or a back-yard, however small or dirty. The animals were tightly bound with cords and laid on a bench; calves hung up alive by their hind-legs and bled without being stunned. With pigs, as soon as the blood for making sausages had been collected, and almost before the animal's cries had ceased, it was thrown, still kicking, into the scalding vat, and the bristles scraped off. For disembowelling the animal was hung up to a wooden hook-frame, which was fixed up in any corner handy, often near a heap of manure or a w.c.; there the carcass was left hanging until it was cut up.

Often the room or yard used for slaughtering had no special entrance, and the cattle were driven through the passages and rooms of the houses to be slaughtered. If the weather were cool, the meat was left hanging in uncleanly slaughter-houses or in the living rooms of houses, even in rooms where sick persons were lying.

Anyone who can read such facts without being seized with a feeling of nausea at the idea of using meat as food must be thoroughly case-hardened.

It is characteristic of the German race to cling to old-established customs, and a rude shock was needed to rouse the public to the necessity of reform. For years no one ventured to make a stand against the revolting state of things we have described. There was grumbling and dissatisfaction, and that was all. The fear of taking energetic steps—a fear fostered by the meat-dealers—was based on the belief that if any alteration were made the price of meat would rise. People hesitated, moreover, to interfere with the butchers' right to manage their business as they pleased.

Other considerations also carried weight, all more or less of a mean and petty order. There can, in fact, be no doubt that nothing would have been done had not the Government taken resolute action in the interest of the whole community as soon as sanitary statistics proved that the existing state of things could not go on without grave danger to the rapidly-increasing population of our towns.

Up to this time no one had had the courage to suggest the building of proper public abattoirs. Every municipality was more or less afraid that such institutions would not pay their way, while the butchers insisted that their business would be greatly hampered by their use—an assertion which was listened to all the more readily because of the wish to avoid spending money.

A circumstance which contributed very largely to the passing of slaughter-house laws was the fact that about this time a remarkably large number of meat-poisoning cases occurred. Numbers of persons were attacked, and in many instances with fatal results.

The carefully-compiled record of these meat-poisoning cases furnished weighty arguments for the abolition of the then existing state of things. We will only quote a few of the more striking instances.

In Bregenz, in the case of a cow which had been slaughtered on account of injuries to the genital canal and the retention of the after-birth (in some cases only broth made of the flesh was consumed), 51 persons were taken violently ill, especially those who had eaten the liver, and 6 persons died. Through eating the flesh of a cow which had been seized with sickness after the birth of its calf, and which had to be destroyed, 84 persons were poisoned, 5 of whom died. In Nordhausen the flesh of a cow, which had been destroyed after suffering from acute diarrhœa and prostration, caused illness in the case of 400 people, 7 of whom failed to recover. In Wurzen 206 persons were attacked with illness, 6 fatally, who had eaten the flesh of a cow which had been slaughtered on account of inflammation of the udder and paralysis of the hind quarters.

At Middleburg, in Holland, of 349 persons who suffered from eating *fresh* liver sausages of unknown origin, 6 died.

At Andelfingen, on the occasion of a choral festival, 450 persons were attacked after eating veal; 10 died. In the same way, at a similar festival at Kloten, 591 persons who had taken part in the festival, besides others who had consumed meat from the same slaughter-house, 657 in all, were seized with illness, and 16 died, the cause in this case being the flesh of a calf which had been slaughtered when almost dead from disease.

At Reichenau, in Saxony, 150 persons were attacked after eating the flesh of a cow which had suffered from inflammation of the stomach; 4 died.

At Arfenreuth 300 persons were poisoned by the flesh of a cow which had been destroyed when suffering from disease; 2 died.

At Bischofswerda 100 persons suffered after eating sausages made from the flesh of a diseased cow.

In Kempen also there was a case of meat-poisoning due to the consumption of sausages; 100 persons were attacked and 6 died.

Statistics show that between the years 1870 and 1880 there were 55 cases of meat-poisoning, involving 2,700 cases of illness and about 96 deaths.

These figures speak volumes as to the necessity for slaughter-house control and proper meat inspection. In addition to cases of ordinary meat-poisoning *trichinæ* epidemics, which often occurred before trichinæ inspection was officially instituted, alarmed the public, and justly so.

On account of these occurrences the cry made itself more and more distinctly heard that it was time for slaughter-houses to be controlled in such a way as to put an end to such a state of things.

Then, at last, the public was made aware of nuisances silently endured for years past caused by the proximity of private slaughter-houses to human dwellings, the cries of slaughtered animals, and the nauseous smells emitted from butchers' premises, which poisoned the air of our towns.

The frequently-recurring epidemics of typhoid were rightly ascribed to the pollution of the ground by slaughter-house refuse, and it was shown that cholera gained a firm foothold in towns where the soil was tainted by the same cause.

The protests raised by medical men and members of the Society of Veterinary Surgeons, which had been previously disregarded, were now listened to with more attention. Committees were appointed to inquire into the origin and spread of epidemics, and soon issued recommendations to municipal and legislative authorities as to the best methods of reform. Suggestions were made as to the improvement of the system of drainage, the question of the proper water-supply was raised, but the main point was universally seen and acknowledged to be the removal of the slaughtering establishments outside the city boundaries.

In many cases the recommendations made were immediately acted on. The building of public abattoirs was resolved on, and the resolution carried out without opposition. In the majority of cases, however, stern measures had to be employed before the desired reform could be effected. The method which was found to be the most efficacious consisted in a series of unexpected visits of inspection paid to private slaughter-houses and butchers' premises at short intervals. In this way abundant evidence was collected as to the existence of abuses. Diseased meat, either whole carcasses or portions of carcasses, was seized, and the offending parties, who were guilty of endangering the lives of their fellow-citizens, severely punished.

With regard to the structural arrangements of slaughter-houses, the authorities insisted on immediate improvements being made, and passed by-laws necessitating thorough and often costly alterations, in some cases going so far as to close, either temporarily or permanently, premises which were particularly insanitary.

As at the same time the municipalities generally put forward the project of building a public abattoir, the butchers in most cases gave up the idea of improving and modernising their existing premises, and joined in the scheme.

Thorough and effective reform, however, could not be carried out even by such measures as we have described, until finally the matter was made a subject for legislation.

This occurred after no great lapse of time in the year 1868, when a law was passed, not only urging the erection of public abattoirs in the interest of the public health, but making their use compulsory when erected.

We shall have occasion to thoroughly examine this statute in a subsequent chapter. For the moment we merely wish to point out that this law did not become of real value till the passing of a supplementary law in 1881. The original law was, in fact, evaded to a great extent by the greatly-increased importation of meat from a distance, which had been subjected to only superficial inspection, or possibly none at all.

This had the effect of nullifying the protection afforded to the public by the preparation of meat in public abattoirs, and also made it difficult for these institutions, which had often been erected at considerable expense, to pay their way.

In cases where the health of a town was endangered by insanitary private slaughter-houses, it was possible to put an end to the nuisance by simply closing these establishments.

There were, however, private slaughtering premises to which no objection could be raised on sanitary grounds, the suppression of which was, however, required if a thorough reform was to be carried out. In cases of this kind there was no course left to the magistrates but to pay compensation.

It may well be supposed that the butchers did not miss such an excellent opportunity of making money quickly, and in most instances claimed exorbitant sums which it would have been impossible to pay.

In many cases where no amicable arrangement could be come to, arbitrators were appointed under a Government official, who soon settled disputed points.

The following figures show what amounts were claimed, and the figures appended in brackets are the sums actually paid by the municipalities:

At Stolp £4,500 was claimed (£243 paid); at Crimmitschau £1,241 claimed (£298 paid); at Wittstoch £86 claimed (£42 paid); at Ohlan £625 claimed (£110 paid); at Nicolai £1,192 claimed (£155 paid); at Gratz

£1,500 claimed (£160 paid); at Glückstadt £1,250 claimed (£270 paid); at Görlitz £3,367 claimed (£459 paid); at Ruppin £1,545 claimed (£216 paid); at Gnesen £2,000 claimed (£770 paid); at Colberg £700 claimed (£100 paid); at Dortmund £1,500 claimed (£690 paid); at Iserlohn £1,498 claimed (£90 paid); at Weissenfels £1,000 claimed (£200 paid); at Kiel £12,500 claimed (£950 paid); at Eschweiler £750 claimed (£200 paid); at Remscheid £2,500 claimed (£450 paid); at Wesel £1,690 claimed (£238 paid); at Frankfurt-on-the-Oder £9,500 claimed (£1,400 paid); at Stendal £1,690 claimed (£750 paid); at Hanover £680 claimed (£140 paid); at Naumburg £3,370 claimed (£365 paid); at Magdeburg £19,350 claimed (£2,100 paid); at Kassel £12,700 claimed (£1,050 paid).

The comparison afforded by the above figures makes it clear that the exorbitant claims frequently put forward were very considerably reduced. One more case shall be quoted as being particularly instructive.

A butcher claimed compensation from the municipality to the extent of £1,500: £300 was awarded in satisfaction of the claim. The butcher carried his case against the municipality through all the courts, with the result that the supreme court awarded him £100 compensation, but sentenced him to pay four-fifths of the costs, which amounted to considerably more than the sum received for compensation. Actual results showed that on an average 10 per cent. of the amount claimed was paid. We must not omit to mention that in many towns no compensation was demanded, because the butchers were intelligent enough to hail the establishment of an abattoir as a welcome improvement which would further their own interests.

At the present day Germany has in round numbers 900 public abattoirs. These are established in all the larger towns without exception, and even in small communities numbering as few as 1,250 inhabitants, well-arranged public slaughter-houses are found.

In recent times hardly a week has passed without some new establishment of the kind being opened. The good example set by the towns in erecting abattoirs has not been without its influence on private slaughter-houses still existing in the country districts, and many of these have in the course of years been so improved by the adoption of modern appliances and improved structural arrangements, that they may almost be regarded as miniature abattoirs.

The requirements of modern sanitation are scrupulously complied with in obedience to police regulations; the flooring is impervious, the water-supply ample, and proper arrangements made for drainage. In places where abattoirs are not supplied with a cold storage chamber, it has frequently been the case that butchers have built their own cold store—small and simple it may be, but yet fulfilling all the necessary conditions for the proper preservation of meat without using ice for the purpose.

How the Attention of the Public was Directed to the Question of Slaughter-House Reform in Germany.

The first movement towards the improvement of the slaughter-house system in Germany originated in the large and wealthy towns. These towns were not only the first to raise the question of reform, but they were the first to erect establishments, the creation of which was a death-blow to the previously existing system.

We all know how hard it is to make a beginning, and we need feel no surprise that the first abattoirs built fell

PUBLIC SLAUGHTER-HOUSE AT OFFENBACH, FIRST USED IN 1832.

far short of perfection. For one thing, there was no model to work on. For another, at the time we speak of the science of public sanitation had not reached that stage of development which it has to-day.

In those days the erection of an abattoir was an event which attracted the attention of the civilised world.

At the present day those early buildings stand like the grizzled veterans of some hard-fought war, whose aged and scar-seamed frames hardly win the honour of a passing glance.

The present generation does not give a thought to the difficulties which beset the inauguration of those early abattoirs, nor to the continual alterations and extensions which had to be made to keep them abreast of the times, nor to the anxious struggle for their very existence which had to be waged until their cause was championed by the law.

And yet even at the present day there are some of those abattoirs still standing which command the admiration of professional experts, although, in comparison with the most modern establishments, they are, so to say, mere relics of the past. But the watchword has been 'Forward.' Improvements have been made in all directions, new systems devised and carried out, and in this field, as in others, the old has been superseded by the new.

For one thing we have to thank the earliest abattoirs, and that is for proving that these institutions can be self-supporting, that they can pay their way without extraneous assistance. And if this was possible under a regime which gave them no assistance, it was shown to be doubly possible when they were backed up by the strong arm of the law. The first successful experiments induced other towns to emulate the example set, in the hope of deriving revenue from the abattoir for the municipality, as had been the case elsewhere.

In many cases, no doubt, hygienic principles may have been a secondary consideration, and the real motive municipal gain.

What particular cause helped the spread of the public slaughter-house system is immaterial; the important fact is that the system did spread. Public attention having been directed to the profit which came from public slaughter-houses, more interest was felt in slaughter-house reform; and when the most conclusive proof was given by statistics that abattoirs were also a means towards the introduction of a perfectly hygienic system, another, if not the first inducement, was given for their establishment.

The adoption of various improvements in abattoirs as time went on had the effect of re-organising their construction, their arrangement, and their methods of working. New establishments equipped with the latest improvements roused the envy of municipalities which only possessed antiquated abattoirs, and the need was felt of placing such establishments on a footing more in keeping with modern requirements.

The advent of the cold-storage system, while facilitating the carrying out of hygienic measures, caused abattoirs to be remodelled on an entirely new plan. The introduction of overhead transport reduced the size of the building, and rendered it less costly to construct. Supplementary departments were added with a view to increased cleanliness, buildings for storing hides, for drying blood, for cleansing intestines, for destroying or disinfecting diseased matter, even for supplying vaccine, were added to the original abattoir, and the existence of the last-mentioned department is sufficient guarantee of the high standard of cleanliness in the whole establishment.

And although burdened with these additions the abbatoirs still paid their way—in fact, made better returns than previously. There is no authentic record of an abattoir requiring assistance from the rates to support it. Each and all of them have been self-supporting, paying interest on the capital outlay, and furnishing a sinking fund to wipe off the original debt. In many cases even they have helped to bring about a reduction of the rates.

The facts which we have previously stated show how necessary it was that the question of slaughter-house reform should be faced; and if in so doing a certain amount of risk was incurred, all the more honour is due to those who did not shirk the responsibility.

Any taint or pollution resulting from slaughtering operations was finally eliminated by the spread of the cold-storage system which superseded the use of ice cellars for preserving meat.

The cold store, moreover, reconciled the butcher to the strict regulations enforced in the public abattoirs. By means of it butchers were enabled not only to keep their meat from perishing, but also to preserve it in such an admirable condition as to attract custom and please the most fastidious palate. The cold store is of twofold benefit to the public. Firstly, by abolishing the old-fashioned method of storing meat on ice; and, secondly, by supplying the customer with an article of diet in a perfectly sanitary condition. The consumer, naturally, is quick to notice what tradesmen serve him best in this respect.

We will discuss the other commercial advantages accruing to the butcher from the use of the cold store when treating this subject more at length.

The addition of the cold store—and even in small and modestly-equipped establishments it is not lacking—was the final touch which made the public abattoir complete.

If we ask ourselves at this point what it was that more than anything else tended to make slaughter-house reform a burning question, we shall find an answer in the ever-increasing desire of the intelligent public to have all flesh food subjected to a system of strict supervision. The alarm occasioned by repeated cases of meat-poisoning found expression in the demand for a properly-regulated system of meat inspection. It was admitted on all hands that meat inspection, even of a desultory kind, was an advance on the past, when no inspection of any sort was practised. At the same time, it was soon recognised that no inspection could be efficiently carried out except in public abbatoirs, and that here the supervision was far more thorough than in the case of slaughtering operations conducted on private premises. In abattoirs also the law insisted that meat inspection should only be exercised by properly qualified veterinary surgeons. This latter regulation was an absolute guarantee that the inspection would be carried out efficiently.

Germany was the first country to have scientifically-trained meat inspectors and to employ their services. These, in their turn, formed a school of practical meat inspectors who were thoroughly trained in the theory and practice of meat inspection, and then sent out to carry on their vocation in accordance with the instruction they had received.

At the present day in the larger towns of Germany none but trained veterinary surgeons are employed in the abattoirs. But besides this it has been resolved that even in small establishments, on account of the greater security afforded, only veterinary surgeons shall be appointed, or at least that any non-scientifically-trained inspectors shall always act under the supervision of fully-qualified surgeons. In addition to the ordinary meat inspectors thousands of trichinosis experts are employed whose special duty it is to examine microscopically the flesh of all swine slaughtered.

Starting with the assumption that meat inspection, if it is to be effective, must be practised by officials who are in an absolutely independent position, it was determined that such officials should be appointed for life, and be granted a pension on retiring.

There can be no doubt that this particular class of official had no easy task to discharge until the butchers became accustomed to strict supervision. Many a refractory subject had to be dealt with before the admirable state of things which exists to-day had been achieved.

From the moment that meat inspection was inaugurated cases of meat-poisoning became a thing of the past. Trichinæ epidemics were no more heard of, and at the present day this system of inspection, costly though it be, works safely and smoothly to the benefit of the community which feels no further anxiety as to its flesh food.

Until recently, however, the state of things we have described did not exist in country districts. Within the last few years there were places where meat inspection, if not absolutely unknown, could not be called systematic. In fact, it was carried out in such a way that it might as well not have been exercised at all. But a great advance has been made by the passing of the Imperial Meat Inspection Act. This measure has swept away with one stroke of the pen all special enactments in force in different petty states, and has made the system of meat inspection one and the same throughout the length and breadth of the empire. But the Act has not merely established uniformity in the methods of inspection, but also in the manner in which inspectors are to be trained.

The old-fashioned inspector of the past who was no longer in touch with modern ideas has been superseded, and replaced by men trained according to the latest methods. Courses of lectures have been held in all German abattoirs to give technical instruction to meat inspectors and trichinosis specialists, and those who have attended such courses not less than four weeks have had to show, by passing an examination before the State medical authorities, that they are competent to exercise their official functions. The salaries of meat inspectors have been increased by supplementary regulations of the new law, and at the present day, only a short time after it has come into force, we have a special staff of thoroughly trained inspectors distributed throughout the whole country.

Thus, by a process of evolution which has gone on for centuries, the condition of things has been arrived at which exists in Germany to-day. But the achievements of the last thirty years entirely eclipse all that was done before.

It is not, however, only in Germany that reforms have been effected. In Austria, Switzerland, Belgium, Holland, and France similar changes, though perhaps less thorough, have been carried out.

In the erection of public abattoirs the countries we have mentioned are not far behind those of Germany. In Austria most admirably arranged public slaughter-houses have been built, and similar establishments are to be found in Switzerland, Holland, Denmark, Belgium, and France. In Russia there has been an attempt to introduce universal meat inspection, at any rate in abattoirs; and though these institutions do not exist in large numbers at present, yet such as are to be found are of the latest design. Hungary possesses several excellent public slaughter-houses, particularly the abattoirs for pigs in Buda-Pesth. Servia and Roumania have built slaughter-houses within the last few years which might serve as a model to other countries; and in Sweden the first public abattoir has been recently opened.

We will not speak here of the gigantic slaughtering establishments to be found in America. They are constructed, not with any idea of furthering public hygiene, but, in a purely commercial spirit, to facilitate slaughtering operations on the largest possible scale.*

Reasons which should Recommend the Abattoir to the Butcher.

Before dealing with the question of opposition to public slaughter-houses, which is the subject of our next chapter, we should wish to say something of the reasons which should make butchers—who are generally opposed to public slaughter-houses—inclined to welcome their introduction.

The practical reasons which make a public abattoir of benefit to butchers are numerous. Modern abattoirs are built expressly for the purpose they are intended for, with abundant air, light, and space, while water is supplied so as to secure the greatest possible cleanliness. As a result we have such system and cleanliness as were never dreamed of before. An abattoir which is properly worked will have its own well-trained staff for slaughtering operations, and thus not only will animals be spared unnecessary pain, but butchers will be able to do their work with a much smaller staff than was previously possible.

The butcher can buy any number of cattle which may

* This passage was written before anything had been heard of the American meat scandals.

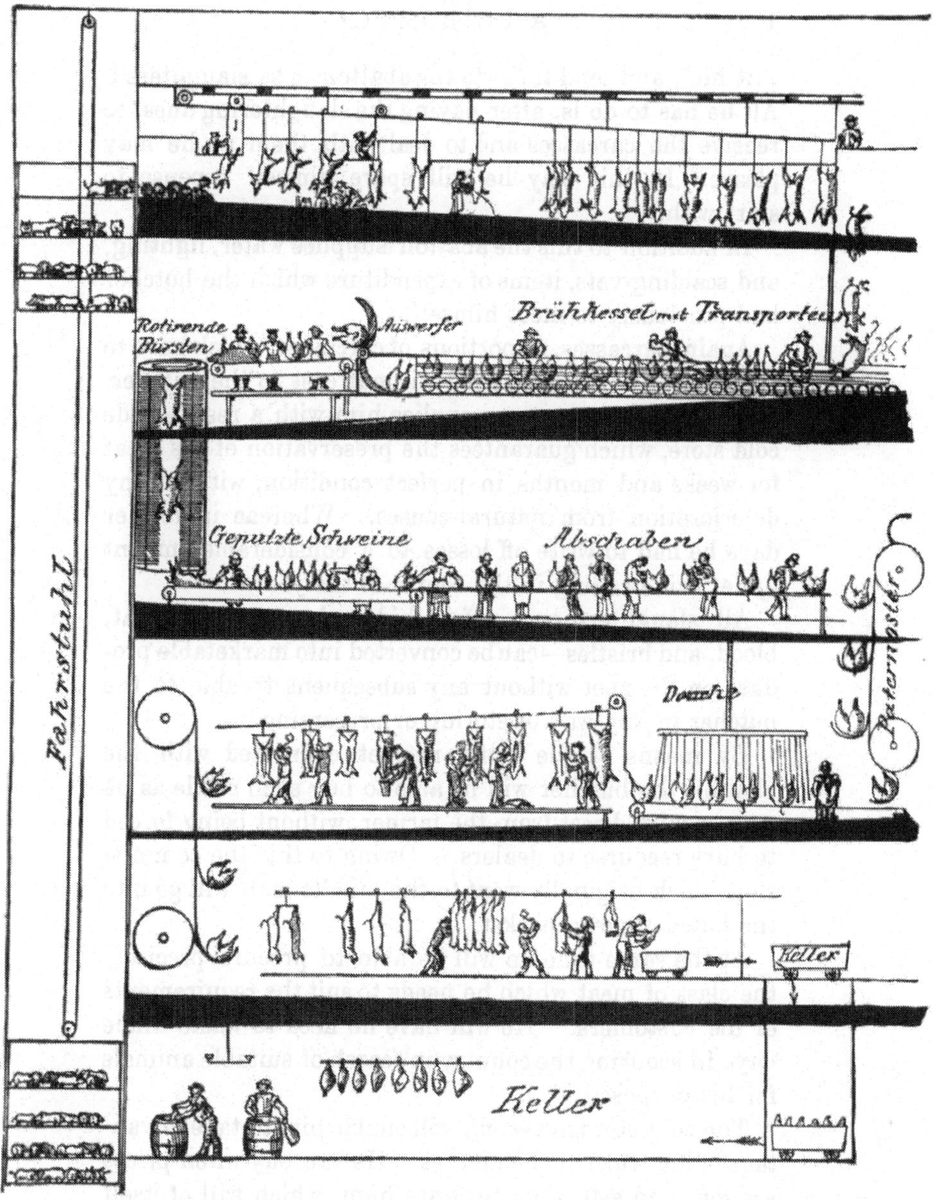

GERMAN PRINT OF CHICAGO PORK FACTORY, SHOWING SLAUGHTERING AND SCALDING OF SWINE, ROTARY BRUSHES FOR REMOVING BRISTLES, ETC.

suit him, and send them to the abattoir to be slaughtered. All he has to do is, after paying the slaughtering dues, to receive the carcasses and to deal with them as he may please. In this way he will spare himself expense to start with.

In addition to this the abattoir supplies water, lighting, and scalding-vats, items of expenditure which the butcher had previously to meet himself.

Again, carcasses, or portions of carcasses, which have to be disposed of are destroyed without cost to the butcher. The abattoir, moreover, supplies him with a ready-made cold store, which guarantees the preservation of his meat for weeks and months in perfect condition, without any deterioration from natural causes. Whereas in former days he had to write off losses to a considerable amount under this heading in the course of the year.

All slaughter-house offal—hides, horns, hoofs, fat, blood, and bristles—can be converted into marketable produce on the spot without any subsequent trouble to the butcher in any way of storing or preserving.

By means of the cattle market connected with the abattoir the butcher will be able to buy such cattle as he may require direct from the farmer, without being forced to have recourse to dealers. Owing to this the commission which originally went to the middle-man will go into the butcher's own pocket.

At the same time he will be able to procure precisely the class of meat which he needs to suit the requirements of his customers. He will have no need to waste whole days in scouring the country in search of suitable animals for his purpose.

The cold-storage system will enable him to take advantage of any turn of the market. He can buy when prices are low, and sell when they are high, which will of itself be of enormous advantage to him.

Cattle brought in from the country, either by rail or on foot, the butcher can have safely housed at minimum

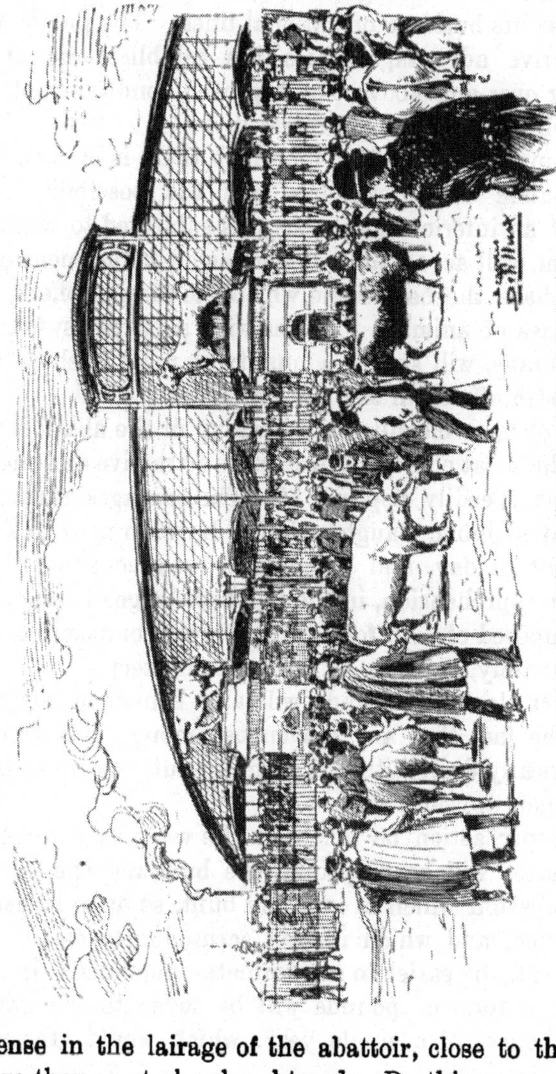

CATTLE MARKET, AUDERLECHT, BELGIUM.

expense in the lairage of the abattoir, close to the spot where they are to be slaughtered. By this means cattle reach their destination without being a source of danger or annoyance to anyone.

The above advantages will strike any butcher who conducts his business on rational lines. The public also will derive advantages from the establishment of an abattoir over and above the improved conditions of life to which we have already referred.

The mutual inspection for which there is opportunity in a public slaughter-house, and the possibility that meat of an inferior quality may be subjected to scathing criticism, will act on the butchers as an inducement only to purchase the best cattle which the market offers. A high class of animals, together with a proper system of cold storage, will supply a quality of meat such as has never been offered in the market before.

The obvious cleanliness prevailing in the abattoir will make the meat offered for sale more attractive and ensure its being speedily disposed of. The sausages manufactured at a public slaughter-house have no need to shun the light of day, and purchasers may consume them without apprehension, in the full knowledge of what they are composed of. In former days their composition was —fortunately, perhaps—a profound mystery.

The cattle-dealer's trade will also benefit, principally from the fact that any epidemics among cattle will be energetically dealt with and stamped out as soon as they make their appearance.

If proper action be taken by the veterinary surgeons the disease will be nipped in the bud, and the lairage of an abattoir which is carefully built, so as to be easily disinfected, and which is kept scrupulously clean, will make it all the easier to exterminate epidemics. In this way thousands of pounds will be saved to the nation in the course of a single year, which would otherwise be wasted through loss of live-stock and diminished food and milk supply.

We need insist no further on the advantages derived from public abattoirs. Facts speak for themselves; and it is almost incomprehensible that in the progressive age in which we live the establishment of such beneficial institutions should be opposed. That this, however, is the case the following chapter will show.

CHAPTER II

OPPOSITION TO PUBLIC ABATTOIRS

It is a remarkable fact that even where the inhabitants of a town are men of intelligence and progressive ideas, the mere suggestion of building a public abattoir is sufficient to call into existence two hostile parties, the one in favour of and the other opposed to the scheme.

In every case we find that the erection of an abattoir is regarded as a most momentous undertaking, which has to be approached with as much solemnity as though the particular abattoir in question were the first ever built upon this earth. Both those who are competent to express an opinion on the matter and those who are not—the latter being naturally in the majority—shake their heads over the question with an air of superhuman sagacity, and discuss every aspect of the case with consequential gravity.

Committee after committee is appointed, and every member feels that it is incumbent on him to display his wisdom (?) by interpolating some trivial suggestion lest the question should be settled in too simple and straightforward a manner. Valuable assistance is thus rendered and great evils averted!

A deputation is then appointed to visit the slaughter-houses in other towns, the members of which commission, as experience shows, having no distinct idea of what is required, evince a singular aptitude for visiting such abattoirs as are least adapted to serve as a model for the one it is proposed to erect. In a word, another example is given of the truth of the old proverb, 'Parturiunt montes,' etc.

A commission of inquiry conducted in such an aimless and haphazard manner seldom makes a unanimous report, and still less frequently has any definite plan to submit to the municipal authorities.

In the meanwhile the opposition has ample time to marshal its forces, and the most sanguine optimist will have to admit that the measure, beneficial though it be, will only be passed after a fiercely-contested struggle.

A statement, which we have no hesitation in making, and which we can bring ample evidence to prove, is that the butchers are the life and soul of the opposition. They are secretly afraid that they may have high dues to pay, that certain methods which they practised in private may be put a stop to, and that they may be interfered with in the easygoing management of their business.

The general public, influenced by the butchers and their followers, oppose the new scheme because they have been convinced (the source of such conviction is not far to seek !) that the abattoir dues will cause the price of meat to rise.

The responsible authorities hesitate to proceed from fear of incurring a heavy debt which they may be unable to discharge or pay interest on, and also because they shrink from the unpopularity and unpleasantness which decisive action on their part will provoke.

It may, perhaps, be interesting at this point to carefully examine the various arguments which are urged against the establishment of abattoirs, and in this way to cut the ground from under the feet of those who oppose such institutions.

To begin with, then, any fear on the score of high slaughter-house dues is entirely without foundation.

Let the butcher calculate the cost of running his private slaughter-house, and remember that all the conveniences to which we have referred in a previous chapter, and which the butcher did not obtain gratis on his own premises, will be supplied in the abattoir more cheaply than at home, on account of the large number whose wants are catered for. Moreover, all arrangements and appliances at a public abattoir will be far more perfect than in a private slaughter-house.

Again, the butchers must remember that when all private slaughter-houses have been closed, the ground on which they stood can be utilised for other purposes, and either sold for building-sites or used as such by the owners themselves.

Any dislike that a butcher may at first feel for the official supervision of an abattoir will wear off in a few weeks, when he has learned to appreciate the advantages and conveniences for his work which are to be found in such an establishment. He will even ask himself why such an admirable system was not introduced earlier, and wonder that he ever felt inclined to oppose it.

The need of effective supervision is what causes the public to insist so emphatically on the establishment of abattoirs. The public has endured the evils of the old system long enough. People will no longer be content to consume meat which has not been subjected to adequate inspection, and will not run the risk of injury to health through want of a system of proper supervision.

Most assuredly, the public is entitled to insist upon its rights, and any objection which the butchers may urge on the ground of compulsory supervision must fall to the ground.

But to return. The municipal authorities themselves, who are urged by their fellow-townsmen to erect an abattoir, are far from ready to adopt the proposed innovation.

Almost always, when the building of an abattoir is discussed, the same objections are raised: 'We have no money for such a purpose;' 'We cannot think of such a thing;' 'Even were funds forthcoming, no one would guarantee that the institution would pay its way.' But if a town has no funds at hand it has the means of raising funds, namely, credit; and the money required will be the more easily obtained because it can be shown that in every single case public abattoirs, whether large or small, have been able to pay their way. We are, of course, supposing that their use is made compulsory. This is a *sine qua non*. Without such compulsion the financial success of an abattoir is never assured. Even if some sacrifices have to be made in order to redeem vested rights, such sacrifices ought to be willingly made in the cause of public hygiene, with a view to introducing compulsory public slaughtering.

No considerations of expense ought to prevent the necessary steps being taken. Regard for what is due to all classes and all industries ought to be an incentive to energetic action, whether unpleasantness may result, whether difficulties may be purposely raised on political, religious, or personal grounds, to hinder or prevent the execution of the proposed reform. Until the final victory is won the struggle should be carried on with unremitting zeal.

Before the terrors of a threatened rise in the price of

meat the public has no need to tremble. The threatened rise may possibly take place, and, in fact, in most places, when an abattoir is first opened, such a rise is attempted.

Justification for anything of the kind there is absolutely none, and very soon we notice that the good friend of the public, 'competition,' shatters any vain hopes that may have been indulged in, and that permission on the part of the town to import meat from a distance speedily places matters on a proper footing again.

In every instance it is noticed that a factitious rise in prices is shortly followed by a return to normal rates. Statistics even show that in many German towns prices have been lower after the opening of an abattoir than they were before.

A Swedish veterinary surgeon of Stockholm, of the name of Kjerrulf, took the trouble to send out inquiry forms to 560 towns possessing abattoirs. The answers received he embodied in a little book, which deserves careful perusal by municipal authorities who are about to build an abattoir. The evidence contained in this little book is sufficient to refute any theory of a rise in the price of meat. Out of a total of 560 towns applied to, 388 returned replies. Of these, 261 towns declared that as a result of the compulsory use of the abattoir and compulsory meat inspection, the price of meat had not been raised.

In the case of twenty-two towns prices rose temporarily, but, owing to the factors above referred to, soon reverted to their normal level. In many cases it was alleged that the temporary rise was due, not to the abattoir, but to other causes, notably the scarcity of live-stock.

The questions, or rather, the answers received, may be classified as follows :

83	from	towns of	from	1,000	to	6,000	inhabitants.
102	,,	,,	,,	5,000	,,	10,000	,,
57	,,	,,	,,	10,000	,,	15,000	,,
32	,,	,,	,,	15,000	,,	20,000	,,
37	,,	,,	,,	20,000	,,	30,000	,,
19	,,	,,	,,	30,000	,,	40,000	,,
12	,,	,,	,,	40,000	,,	50,000	,,
3	,,	,,	,,	50,000	,,	60,000	,,
6	,,	,,	,,	60,000	,,	70,000	,,
6	,,	,,	,,	70,000	,,	80,000	,,
1	,,	,,	,,	80,000	,,	90,000	,,
7	,,	,,	,,	90,000	,,	150,000	,,
2	,,	,,	,,	150,000	,,	200,000	,,
8	,,	,,	,,	200,000	,,	1,000,000	,,

The inquiries made were in the following terms:

1. Has the establishment of an abattoir and compulsory meat inspection raised the price of meat?

2. Has the abattoir been able to pay interest on the capital expended on it?

In many cases it is obvious, from the answers, that the price of meat went *down* after the introduction of compulsory meat inspection, or that at any rate there was a relative reduction of price, taking into consideration the improved quality of the meat sold owing to competition among the butchers.

(The reports sent in from Cottbus, Dortmund, Hulmbach, Meran, Remscheid, Tilsitt, and Gardelegen bear on this point.)

Many towns state explicitly that the cost of meat inspection is so slight that no increase of price on this ground is in the least justifiable.

To the inquiry as to whether public slaughter-houses are a financial success, the reply was unanimously in the affirmative. Ever since municipalities have been empowered by law to make public slaughtering and meat inspection compulsory, they have been eager to establish public abattoirs. We may well ask, therefore, whether so large a number of abattoirs would have been built in a space of time comparatively short, had not experience abundantly proved that such institutions are financially sound ?

The author finally sums up the purport of the various answers received in the following statements :

1. Meat is not rendered dearer by compulsory public slaughtering and meat inspection.

2. Public abattoirs are always able to pay interest on the original outlay.

3. Any rise in the price of meat which may be noticed, is really due to the relation between supply and demand. Such rises are to be noticed before an abattoir has been established.

4. The quality of meat always improves after an abattoir has been opened, therefore in a certain sense the price of meat is lowered.

5. The price of meat often goes up directly an abattoir is opened. The butchers attempt to bring about such a rise. In consequence, however, of competition and the greater amount of meat imported when prices are raised, they soon revert to their former level.

6. The price of meat in towns where public slaughtering and meat inspection are enforced by law, is not higher than in neighbouring towns where no such system of compulsion exists.

7. The butchers have as much freedom in the exercise of their vocation as formerly, since everyone who complies with the regulations of the abattoir and pays the fixed tariff for its use, is fully entitled to slaughter or have slaughtering performed there.

On the strength of the above statements we feel

justified in hoping that the opponents of the abattoir system may desist in future from bringing forward those oft-quoted arguments which are so dear to them, and may abandon their hostility to one of the greatest measures of hygienic reform which the present age has known.

At the same time, the friends of such reform must not base their plea on any questionable data. Supported by the above statistics collected in Germany, they can bring overwhelming evidence to prove that their statements are as much borne out by facts as those of their opponents are unfounded.

We must also call attention to the fact that in the case of other countries, besides Germany, all developments of the public slaughter-house system had to be based on one uniform principle laid down by the Government. In this way only can such desirable results be realised as have been undoubtedly obtained. Again, the main statute must be further supplemented by local by-laws, which not only lay down regulations for the use of the abattoir when built, but also exact rules for the internal routine of the establishment.

It would never occur to any municipality to erect a public abattoir at—as is frequently the case—enormous expense, without being fully convinced that the institution will pay its way. Such a conviction will be based, firstly, on the possibility of making the use of the abattoir compulsory; secondly, on a consideration of the probable extent of slaughtering operations as indicated by statistics as to meat consumption; thirdly, on a calculation of expenditure and receipts, or what we may call the prospective balance-sheet of the abattoir.

No injustice is done by conferring on municipalities

the power to make public slaughtering compulsory. A precedent in this respect has long since been established by the butchers themselves. The financial success of the German guild slaughter-houses built by the butchers was ensured by making their use compulsory, and no butcher was allowed to slaughter except on the guild premises.

There are at the present time in Germany about sixty abattoirs which are not municipal property, but belong to guilds of butchers. The existence of such guild slaughter-houses belonging to the butchers themselves, and the high dividends which they pay yearly to the shareholders, are the clearest proof that the objections raised to the abattoir system by butchers are neither sincere nor deserving of consideration. No guild slaughter-house in Germany has ever been known to be such a financial failure as to have to go into liquidation: quite the contrary. Recently, indeed, certain towns (Stuttgart and Dresden) which, through a short-sighted policy, had allowed the butchers to build their own abattoirs, were obliged, owing to altered circumstances, to purchase these premises themselves, and to atone for the folly of a past generation at great financial cost by buying the butchers out. Even when this has been done, and vested rights have been redeemed, the town has only acquired the right to build its own abattoir; for in most cases the existing premises are so far from fulfilling modern requirements that they have to be pulled down and rebuilt. Nothing, therefore, has been gained except the right to build the abattoir.

If, therefore, even under such unfavourable conditions as we have described, municipalities are prepared to build abattoirs which will cost far more than is usually the case—if, for instance, at the present time the city of Dresden is engaged in erecting an abattoir which is to cost £1,000,000 sterling, and to eclipse anything of the kind which has been built hitherto—this fact alone is sufficient to prove that under normal conditions the financial success of an abattoir is beyond all possible doubt.

CHAPTER III

LAWS BEARING ON PUBLIC SLAUGHTER-HOUSES

In the following section of this work we shall give a brief statement of the German slaughter-house laws:

1. Any community which has erected a public abattoir may decree that within the boundaries of the whole community, or any part of it, the slaughtering of all or any species of cattle, together with certain subsidiary occupations connected therewith, shall be exclusively carried on in the public abattoirs.

2. After the erection of a public abattoir, a local by-law may enact that all cattle admitted into it are to be examined by qualified experts both before and after being slaughtered.

3. The above enactments must be ratified by the Local Government Board. The law prohibiting slaughtering to be performed elsewhere than in the public abattoir comes into force six months after the law has been published, unless a clause has been specially inserted, stipulating that a longer period shall elapse.

4. The community is bound to manage and maintain the public slaughter-house in such a way as to meet local requirements.

5. The corporation has the power to levy dues for the

use of the abattoir and inspection of cattle, which dues shall be fixed for at least one year ahead.

The amount of the dues levied is to be such that the dues for inspection cover the expenses thereby entailed, while the dues for the use of the abattoir must not exceed the amount required for the cost of maintaining the establishment, defraying the current expenses, paying interest on the capital outlay, supplying a sinking fund, and meeting any charges for indemnification which may be incurred.

A higher rate of interest than 5 per cent., or a higher percentage than 1 per cent. for the sinking fund, are not allowable.

6. No one can be refused the use of the public abattoir.

7. Compensation has to be paid by the community to all owners or users of private slaughter-houses in the district for any actual loss which they can show to have been incurred by being prohibited from using their premises for the purpose for which they were originally intended. Claims for compensation on the grounds of interference with, or interruption of, trade will not be entertained.

8. All leases and contracts expire at the end of the period specified above.

9. All owners of private slaughter-houses are bound to notify their claims for compensation to the local government within the specified time, under pain of forfeiting their rights to receive compensation.

The government appoints a commissioner, who, with two assessors, has to try the claim and fix the amount of compensation to be paid. One assessor is appointed by the claimant, the other by the community.

10. The commissioner sends in a report of the proceedings to the government, which publishes its decision on the claims for compensation along with the con-

siderations on which the decision is based, and forwards a copy of the award to each of the parties concerned.

11. An appeal may be lodged against this decision within a period of five weeks.

12. The stipulations contained in the law hold good even when the community has surrendered the right of erecting an abattoir to a third party. The community, however, still remains subject to the obligations imposed by the law.

13. Whoever shall perform slaughtering, or carry on any avocation connected with slaughtering, elsewhere than in the public slaughter-house, shall be liable for each offence to a fine of £3, or imprisonment.

This law came into operation in the year 1868. In course of time, however, it was shown that the action of the law was evaded by having cattle slaughtered outside the district boundaries, and the meat brought into the towns for sale.

In this way the prescribed inspection of meat was often evaded, and the law was supplemented by a further Act in 1881, the purport of which was as follows:

After the establishment of a public slaughter-house, local by-laws may enact—

1. That the flesh of animals not slaughtered in the public abattoir cannot be offered for sale as fresh meat within the city boundaries until it has been examined by experts, for which a sum will be charged, which will be paid into the municipal purse.

2. That in hotels and restaurants fresh meat which has been imported from a distance may not be prepared as food until it has been submitted to similar inspection.

3. That both in public markets and butchers' shops the fresh meat of animals not slaughtered in the public abattoir is to be set apart when offered for sale.

4. That in public markets belonging to the Corporation

only the flesh of animals slaughtered in the public abattoir shall be offered for sale.

5. That persons who follow the vocation of butchers or meat-dealers as their regular profession within the township, may not offer for sale the flesh of animals which, instead of being slaughtered in the public abattoir, have been killed at some slaughtering establishment situated within a certain radius defined by the local by-laws.

6. That imported meat which requires inspection shall be submitted to the inspector, in the case of large cattle in entire quarters, in the case of smaller animals in entire carcasses with all the internal organs intact.

7. Whoever shall slaughter cattle, or who shall carry on any of the avocations specified in the Act, except in the public abattoir, and whoever shall be convicted of not complying with the regulations in the case of imported meat, shall be liable for every offence to a fine of £7 10s. or imprisonment.

Until the Imperial law with regard to meat inspection came into force, it was felt that the Act was not complete, since sausages, dried meats, hams, etc., were not subject to inspection.

It is absolutely essential that the laws regarding public slaughter-houses should be supplemented by one universal Act dealing with meat inspection, which shall hold good for the whole country—and such an Act was passed in 1900.

We have already mentioned that this Act swept away at one stroke all existing petty local regulations regarding meat inspection, and that every township, however small, was thereby compelled to appoint meat inspectors.

Not a particle of meat can now be used for food which has not been inspected. It is remarkable in how short a space of time this Act was introduced; and although veterinary surgeons are far from regarding it as perfect, it is certain that a great step has been made towards ensuring public safety with regard to flesh food.

The law did not come into operation until 1903, on account of the necessity of first training meat inspectors for the whole country. It is evident that a great amount of work had to be got through in preparing the necessary staff for their duties. In all the abattoirs in Germany courses of instruction were held for the benefit of those who wished to qualify themselves for their responsible and arduous profession.

According to a special clause contained in the Act, in addition to the regular staff of inspectors, substitutes had to be trained who should be ready to come forward in case of emergency.

The task of selecting from the candidates who presented themselves to be trained was no light one, as it was necessary only to accept those who from their social standing were in an independent position, and, above all, in no wise amenable to the influence of the butchers. Unless this is insisted on no effective result can be expected from the working of the law.

It may, perhaps, be also of interest to learn the main provisions of the Imperial Meat Inspection Act.

This law prescribes that all domestic animals used for food shall be carefully examined both before and after being slaughtered. It requires all meat inspectors immediately to report if they notice the presence of epidemic disease in the discharge of their duties.

Inspection districts have been formed so that places of minor importance may be grouped together in one district.

Before inspection has taken place, no part of an animal may be removed.

If this, however, has been done, the sub-inspector

may report himself as unable to deal with the case, and call upon the veterinary surgeon to conduct the inspection.

The flesh of diseased animals, or meat which is unfit for food, must be confiscated until further orders concerning it are received from the official veterinary surgeon.

The importation of preserved meat or sausages from abroad is prohibited.

In the case of horses, only qualified veterinary surgeons may conduct the inspection.

Every carcass that has been inspected will be stamped with some conspicuous mark indicating the result of the inspection.

In the case of manufactured meat-foods the introduction of chemical products, such as preserving salts, colouring matter, etc., is absolutely forbidden.

Any contravention of these regulations, if with fraudulent intent, will be punished with six months' imprisonment, or a fine of £75; if due to carelessness, with a fine of £7 10s., or a corresponding term of imprisonment.

In addition to the above Act, the consumer is further protected by the law of May 14th, 1879, relating to traffic in food and provisions, which law still remains in force.

The regulations relating to the carrying out of the Imperial Meat Inspection Act explain the working of the law in every detail, and give the meat inspector exact information as to what cases he is competent to deal with.

A clear distinction is drawn between the fully-qualified veterinary officer and the ordinary inspector, and ample directions are given as to the way in which meat which has been confiscated, or parts of diseased animals, are to be disposed of.

The meat inspectors are also enjoined to keep accurate account of all inspections, and the veterinary officials must supervise the work of the sub-inspectors.

Every precaution has been taken for the protection of the health of the public.

In order to regulate the working hours of the inspectors, and to keep the cost of inspection as low as possible, and in order to make it possible for meat inspectors in the country to combine some other occupation with their duties, certain fixed times of the day have been arranged at which inspections are to be held.

Such is the state of things in Germany to-day. Everywhere we find order, cleanliness, security, and the most thorough supervision.

CHAPTER IV

BUILDING AN ABATTOIR: PRELIMINARY CONSIDERATIONS

1. By whom should the Abattoir be built?

There can be no possible doubt that it is the business of the municipal authorities to improve the sanitary condition of a town. Among such improvements we must count the erection of an abattoir. Consequently, under no possible conditions should the municipal authorities surrender their rights in this matter. It is their business to build the abattoir themselves.

If a sanitary institution of this kind is the property of the town, a pledge is hereby given that its management will be above suspicion, and that proper supervision will be exercised. Moreover, all those who make use of it will have the benefit of the latest modern appliances and improvements, a circumstance which may well reconcile them to the new system.

If, on the other hand, the town cedes its right to build the abattoir, whoever undertakes to do so will be tempted to make money out of the venture, and the municipality may be subsequently blamed, and reasonably so, because the price of meat has risen. A town has often to bitterly regret such short-sighted policy—as we have ourselves seen in Germany—and the amount of money required to buy up an abattoir already built, greatly exceeds, as has been shown, the amount required to build a new one.

In cases where the local authorities make an energetic stand in favour of slaughter-house reform, it has frequently been noticed that the butchers, who were previously the declared opponents of the abattoir system, suddenly veer round, acquiesce in the idea, and *volunteer to build the abattoir themselves.*

Should, however, this proposal (as is only probable) be rejected by the local authorities, the butchers will instantly resume their former hostile attitude. Such tactics betray the real reason of their opposition, which is the fear of having their work subjected to proper supervision. After the struggle has been waged with considerable bitterness on both sides, the party of reform, backed by the more enlightened citizens, usually carries the day.

2. The Best Site for an Abattoir.

The question as to where the new abattoir should be built can generally be answered by giving due weight to certain main considerations which should never be lost sight of. The first of these is that the abattoir should, if possible, be built at the point where any river which flows through the town finally emerges from it. We do not say that the abattoir should stand actually on the banks of the river, for this would often be undesirable on account of possible floods. The approach to an abattoir should not be a steep gradient, and especial care should be taken that the roads by which it is reached are broad and well made.

A further point which should be strongly insisted on, particularly in the case of large towns, is that the abattoir should be in immediate connection with the railway.

The transport of cattle, as well as other traffic, will be greatly facilitated by this arrangement. One great advantage resulting therefrom will be that cattle will no longer be driven through the public streets.

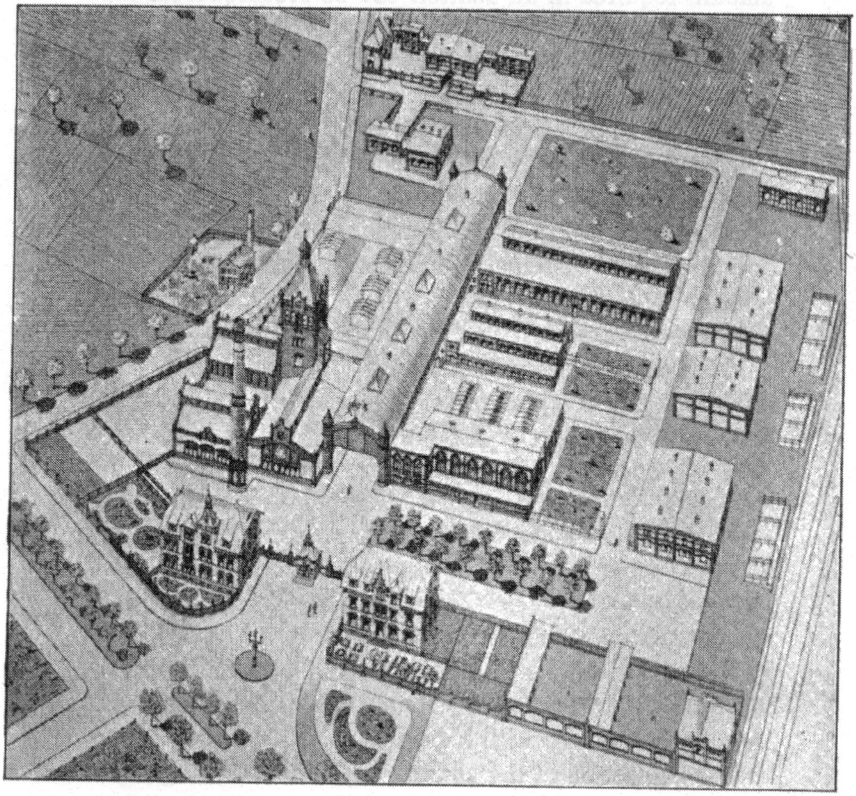

BIRD'S-EYE VIEW OF OFFENBACH NEW ABATTOIR, OPENED IN 1903.

The site selected for the abattoir should be on dry and porous soil, otherwise the construction of cellars which may be eventually required will be made difficult or impossible, and the building expenses be increased.

If the town is already provided with a proper system of drainage, the abattoir should be connected with the main sewer. With regard to the water-supply, it must be decided beforehand whether the very considerable amount required in an abattoir can be procured from the town waterworks, or whether it would not be more advantageous to have a private well. In the latter case trial borings must be made to see whether a sufficient supply can be obtained on the spot.

The proximity of a thickly-populated manufacturing district has a distinct influence on the abattoir, since experience shows that the inhabitants of such districts are the best customers for meat which, though of inferior quality as regards flavour and nourishing properties, is perfectly fit for human food.

If the town possesses electric light, gas, or other public works in which steam power is employed, the abattoir may be worked more cheaply by being situated in their vicinity, since steam for scalding swine, gut-cleansing, etc., may be drawn from the neighbouring works, and save the abattoir the expense of a steam generating plant of its own. The cold-storage machinery may also be worked by electric motors. Moreover, when the question of a public slaughter-house is being settled, the question of a public water-supply and electric lighting may often be settled at the same time, if these matters have not been dealt with before.

The connection of the abattoir with the electric generating station is to be recommended on account of the special fact that the various uses for which electricity is required in an abattoir supplement each other.

In summer little electricity is required for lighting purposes, but a large supply is needed for working the cold store. In winter, on the other hand, there is but little demand for electricity for the cold store, but a heavy call on it for lighting. The fact of being able to make two public institutions co-operate will render both more profitable to the town.

Again, if the wells sunk for the abattoir yield an abundant supply of water, public waterworks may be established in connection with the abattoir.

The requisite plant is already there, and only requires to be extended to meet other demands besides those of the abattoir.

When selecting the site for an abattoir, it is well to bear in mind the possible necessity for purifying the slaughter-house sewage, and there should be sufficient natural fall from the abattoir to the tanks, not to necessitate pumping, as this increases the cost of purification.

An old-fashioned idea which has long been exploded in Germany is that the abattoir should be placed as far outside the town as possible, so as not to be offensive to the public.

It would be a reflection on a modern abattoir to suggest that such an idea has any foundation. Nowadays the theory is that the abattoir should be placed as near as possible to the outskirts of the town, since with modern arrangements no abattoir can be in any way offensive to the neighbourhood. In fact, in many places it is found that rows of dwelling-houses are built in its immediate vicinity, and that ground values in the neighbourhood rise rather than decline, a proof that the idea as to the presence of an abattoir being objectionable is entirely erroneous.

3. Calculating the Size of an Abattoir.

In planning a public slaughter-house the first point to be clear about is the size of the population for which it is required. It would be a great mistake to build an abattoir merely corresponding to the needs of any town. Apart from the fact that as soon as such an institution is opened the slaughtering returns increase, because prior to the establishment of an abattoir many animals are slaughtered without any return being made—that is to say, all record of such slaughtering has been purposely suppressed—apart from this fact, the actual demand for meat will increase. For these reasons the question of enlargement would have shortly to be faced, if due allowance were not made when the abattoir was first built.

It is not overstating the case to say that for a population of 30,000 an abattoir ought to be, *to start with*, big enough for 50,000. It is much easier for too large an establishment to pay the interest on the capital outlay, than for one which has been planned on too small a scale to be altered or enlarged. The best basis of calculation is the number of the population plus one half.

In any case, in view of the fact that the population of a town may increase for a variety of reasons, the possibility of such increase ought to be carefully borne in mind when planning every section of the building. Care should also be taken to arrange that it is possible to make extensions while business is being carried on, and without interfering with the work of the abattoir.

Finally, let the greatest attention be given to the three main desiderata in an abattoir—*air, light, space.*

4. Estimating the Cost of an Abattoir.

By the accurate returns made in Germany regarding the construction of abattoirs, it is shown that the cost for a town of under 20,000 inhabitants is 14s. per head,

KIEL ABATTOIR (FRONT ELEVATION).

without cold store; with cold store, 19s. For a town of more than 20,000, about 15s. 6d.; for a town of more than 100,000, 12s.; in both cases *without* a cold store, which costs an additional 5s. per head.*

Anyone, however, who has even a superficial knowledge of abattoirs will admit that it is difficult to speak authoritatively on the subject of cost. The way in which the work is carried on, the choice of an architect, the cost of materials, and the rate of workmen's wages, which vary in different countries, must all be taken into account. One town takes a pride in having a handsomely-appointed abattoir, another considers that the simplest which can be built is quite expensive enough.

In one case we have a building with an imposing front and the interior walls faced with marble; in another plain brickwork and walls faced with cement. The above figures, therefore, must be considered only to represent the average cost of building an abattoir in Germany, and not as in any way fixing a standard of expense for other countries.

5. Errors to Avoid.

In order to avoid the worst mistakes in building an abattoir it is necessary to have technical advice, and the plans for the building should be laid down in consultation with an expert on abattoir matters. The architect and manager must also co-operate, and only in this way can grave errors be avoided which will otherwise become unpleasantly apparent as soon as the institution is opened. Structural faults are serious, but faults affecting the working of the establishment are far more so.

The chief structural faults arise from neglecting the

* Compare these figures with cost of South Shields abatoir given on p. 57.

three essentials in an abattoir — light, air, space. Narrow passages and low slaughtering-halls are especially objectionable. Nor is it wise to shirk the heavy expense attendant on using first-class materials throughout. Such expenditure is amply compensated for in after-years by the small amount which is required to meet depreciation; whereas where inferior materials are employed, the constant need for repairs is an unpleasant source of expense. If at the outset money is not stinted in order that the abattoir may be substantially built, no fault can be found; but if year after year extra sums are needed for upkeep and repairs, complaints will always be made, and the builder be blamed for not having done his work thoroughly. If, for instance, inferior cement is used for the flooring, it will only last a few years; whereas granite and hard sandstone are practically indestructible.

The thorough ventilation of the slaughtering-halls is another point which should be attended to. In a modern abattoir the air should be so pure that nothing reminds you of the use to which the building is put. The presence of draughts should be scrupulously avoided by properly arranging and connecting the different rooms. The workers in an abattoir are often in profuse perspiration, and cold draughts would be injurious to their health.

In building a slaughter-hall for pigs care should be taken that the steam from the scalding-tanks does not find its way into the hanging-house, as this greatly interferes with the work.

If a cold store is provided, let a hanging-house by all means be built, even if fixed hoists are used, in which case, of course, less space would be required in this room. It is only by having such a room, in which to allow the excess of animal heat to escape that the meat can be preserved in a proper state in the cold store.

In planning the hanging-house especial regard should be had to the possible increase of population, as this is a point in which many such rooms are deficient.

The cold store should not measure more than 9 ft. 10 in. in height, as otherwise more money is required to work it. The working of the cold store always increases the expense of working the abattoir, and therefore all unnecessary space should be saved. On the other hand, no expense should be spared to ensure absolute insulation—*i.e.*, the walls must be non-conducting. Any economy that may be attempted in this respect when the building is being constructed will make itself subsequently felt in the form of higher working expenses, and cannot be remedied without serious interruption of business.

It is advisable to have strict rules and regulations drawn up directly an abattoir is opened, and it should be the business of the controlling officials to insist on these regulations being scrupulously observed.

In building an abattoir, above all, let full attention be given to observing the principles of hygiene. It was hygiene that brought the question of slaughter-house reform to the fore, and every point connected with it should be fully thought out and attended to.

Hygiene is the first object of the abattoir; the second, however, is to provide the butcher with every facility for carrying on his trade. There must be an ample supply of good water, and thorough provision be made for purifying the waste-water, and freeing it from infectious germs. Every part of the abattoir must be built so that it can be easily disinfected, and in this way conduce to the stamping out of any infectious epidemic which may occur.

The superintendents of abattoirs should invariably be veterinary surgeons. In England at the present moment it would be no easy matter to obtain properly qualified officials; for, in the absence of public abattoirs, veterinary surgeons have little opportunity for acquiring the requisite knowledge.

It would be as well, therefore, while the abattoir is in process of building, to send prospective abattoir superintendents abroad, so that they may gain a thorough knowledge of their profession in towns whose population is approximately the same as that of the town in which they will be employed. The mistake should never be made of appointing men who are *not* veterinary surgeons. This mistake has been often made in Germany, and as often bitterly regretted; and at the present time, with few exceptions, all abattoirs are controlled by qualified veterinary surgeons. This fact alone shows how satisfactory the plan has proved.

In Germany, abattoir management has become a special science. It is taught at the Universities, and more advanced instruction is to be gained from technical journals dealing with the subject. No German veterinary surgeon, moreover, would undertake the control of a public abattoir until he had gained a thorough knowledge of its management by familiarising himself with the working of such institutions.

There are various practical reasons for appointing none but veterinary surgeons to direct public abattoirs. To begin with, it is necessary to have a veterinary surgeon armed with official authority in an abattoir, with whom rests the final decision as to whether meat is fit for human food or not. Again, it is necessary to have such an official in case an infectious epidemic should break out. It will be his business to supervise the work of the meat inspectors, who are his subordinates.

A veterinary surgeon will easily master the working of an abattoir, and acquire the requisite knowledge for its management. If, however, a man who had received a merely commercial training were placed at the head of an abattoir, he would never be able to discharge the special duties of a veterinary surgeon, and therefore a veterinary officer would have to be appointed in addition. If, however, both functions are united in the person of the veterinary abattoir-superintendent, working expenses will be reduced.

CHAPTER V

THE GERMAN ABATTOIR

THERE are probably few persons in England at the present moment who, from their personal experience of modern abattoirs, are qualified to instruct the public on the subject.

We will endeavour, therefore, in the following chapters, to describe briefly the modern abattoir as it ought to be. In so doing, we may be able to demonstrate the wide difference which separates the present from the past.

The German abattoir is, up to the present time, the most perfect type of the kind to be found in civilised countries. We are speaking more particularly of recent examples. It has served as a model for neighbouring states to imitate, and that it has risen to this position is due to the following causes.

Firstly, to the passing of the needful laws and enactments. Secondly, to the progressive spirit of our municipalities, who have had the courage and self-sacrifice to initiate reforms; and lastly, to the presence of enlightened public opinion, which insisted that the existing state of things should be improved.

All these different factors have contributed to make the German abattoir what it is. In earlier days, both in larger and smaller towns, things were in a similar condition to what they, unfortunately, are in England to-day. But the smaller towns have imitated the example of the larger, and at the present time we find in every corner of our country pattern abattoirs which, on a larger or smaller scale, may serve as a model for any town, whatever be its size. Millions have been spent on the construction of abattoirs, and the towns which have adorned themselves with these handsome buildings have never had, and will never have, occasion to regret the money expended on them.

According to the plan on which abattoirs are built, two systems are distinguished:

1. The system of separate buildings.
2. The block system.

In the first system, as the name indicates, the principal buildings of the abattoir are separated from each other, and are connected by passages.

In the block system, on the other hand, the object aimed at is as far as possible to bring all the different buildings under one roof.

No proof is needed to show that if air, light, and free space are strictly insisted on the first-named system is the better. At the same time both large and small abattoirs have been built on the block system, in which these three points have been most thoroughly attended to, in so far, that is to say, as the system admits of it. Only with regard to lighting, overhead lights instead of windows must be used if the various rooms are to receive a sufficient supply of daylight.

In towns in which only a small or costly site can be secured, recourse must naturally be had to this system from motives of economy.

If, however, the price of land allows of a fairly extensive area for the abattoir, it will always be found that the system of separate buildings is the better and the more practical.

GERA ABATTOIR (BIRD'S-EYE VIEW).

In every abattoir a distinction must be made between principal and accessory buildings.

The former, again, must be divided into buildings connected with the administration and those connected with the working of the establishment. The accessory buildings are also divided into those which are indispensable and those which are not.

Among principal buildings we may reckon: (1) the manager's quarters; (2) those for the officials and staff of the establishment; (3) the abattoir canteen; (4) the porter's lodge.

Among necessary buildings belonging to the slaughter-house proper are: (1) the slaughtering-hall for large cattle; (2) for small cattle; (3) for pigs; (4) the resting-pens for small cattle and pigs; (5) the lairage for large cattle; (6) stables for butchers' horses; (7) the tripe-house: (8) the manure-house.

Among indispensable accessory buildings are recognised: (1) Slaughter-house for diseased animals; (2) sterilising room; (3) slaughter-house for horses and dogs; (4) condemned meat-room; (5) machine and boiler house; (6) lavatories for butchers and their assistants.

Under this heading may also be included: The cold-store with receiving-room, ice-making department, pickling and sausage-making rooms, the 'Frei-bank,' or certified cooked meat shop for sale of inferior meat, the fat and tallow melting factory, and shed for storing hides with drying-room.

Among accessory buildings which are not indispensable are reckoned: Blood-drying and albumin works, as well as factories for pepsin and chemical food, skin-cleaning works (sausage skins), building containing 'destructor' apparatus, animal lymph laboratory, a milk inspection department, plant for chemical treatment of manure,

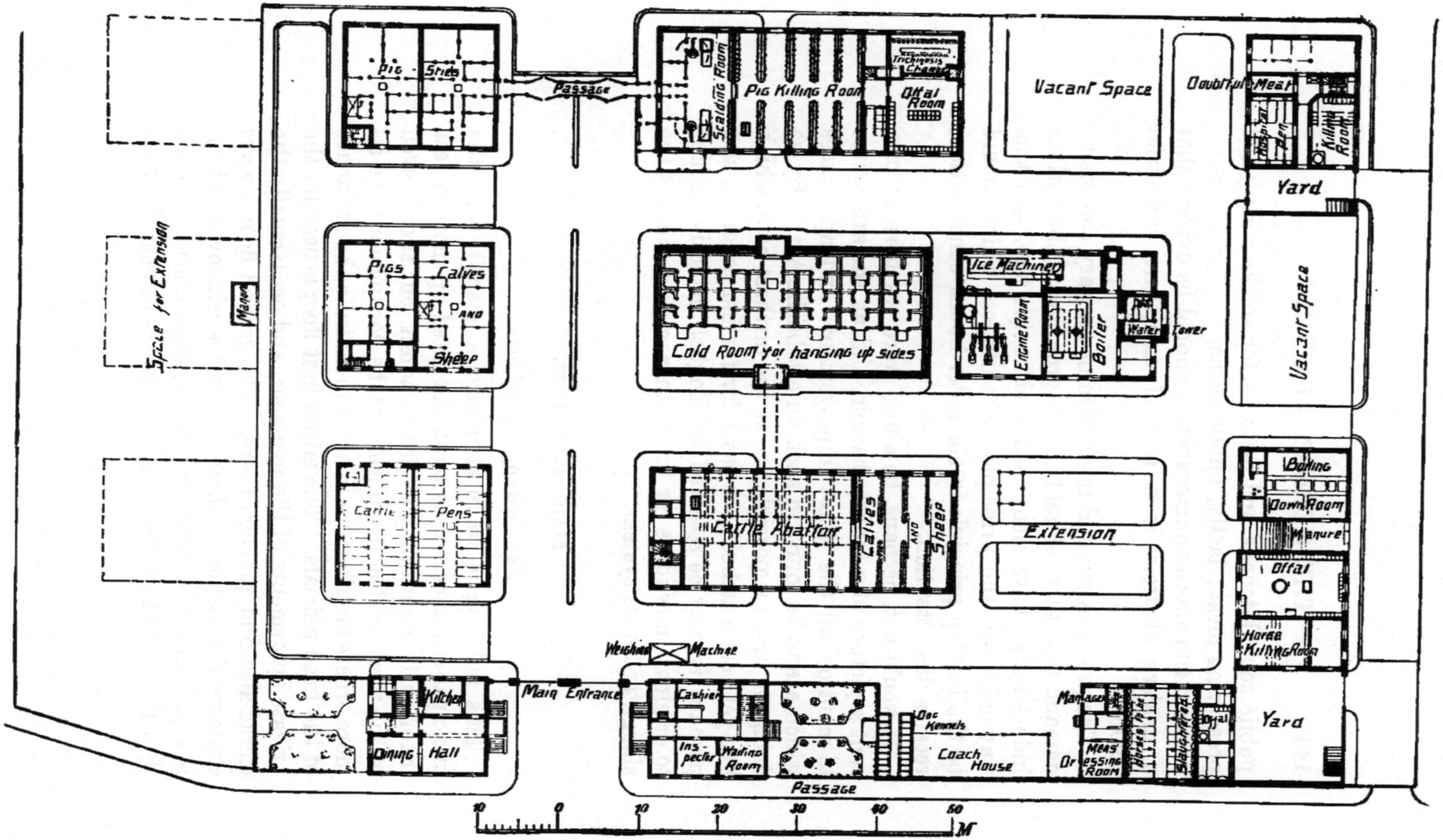

GERA ABATTOIR (GROUND PLAN).

public soup kitchens and factories for smoke curing and preserving meat; lastly, public baths.

From the above enumeration it should be evident that a modern abattoir is a sort of miniature industrial colony.

The preservation and promotion of sanitary conditions demand that there should be this grouping of the various industries we have mentioned, and in this way, and this way only, will the principle of sanitation, which should be the leading principle in slaughter-house construction, receive due attention.

It would not, perhaps, be amiss were we here to present a picture of a model abattoir, and at the same time to mention all the latest improvements and appliances which are to be found in such an establishment. By so doing we make it possible to use the furthest point which has yet been reached as a basis for further progress, and perhaps it may be reserved for English inventive genius to originate new ideas for the further improvement of the slaughter-house system.

Main Buildings.

The Manager's House.

This building is in most abattoirs placed near the principal entrance. It is built and fitted up more or less luxuriously accordingly as funds admit, but should even in the most modest establishment be conspicuous by its more ornate architecture in order to indicate the residence of the head officials. The entire first floor is used for the private apartments of the manager, and occasionally the clerks also find quarters there. The ground floor always contains the cashier's offices, the office window of which is sometimes in a handsome hall—sometimes is reached by a flight of steps from outside. In the newest abattoirs

ABATTOIR AT LA CHAUX DE FONDS, SWITZERLAND (FRONT ELEVATION).

a great point is made of having the cashier's offices elegantly fitted up. In Bamberg there is one, the walls of which are faced with grey glazed tiles, the flooring is red, the partitions of oak, and the lattice nickel-plated. In Plauen the handsomest cashier's office in Germany is to be found.

The weigh-bridge for live animals can be managed from the cashier's office or the porter's lodge.

The manager's offices are simply but completely fitted up, and in recently-built abattoirs there is telephonic communication between these rooms and every part of the establishment. In large abattoirs there is a committee-room for the slaughter-house committee and a library, and also a laboratory for conducting special investigations.

Trimly-kept gardens are laid out round the manager's house, and gardens are also provided elsewhere for the rest of the staff, as this encourages domestic tastes.

If the staff is numerous, larger buildings are erected, in which rooms are assigned to all.

Indispensable Buildings belonging to the Abattoir Proper.

We now come to a second group of buildings—those in which the actual work of the establishment is carried on.

In quite small abattoirs built on a modest scale for towns of 5,000 inhabitants or less, it is generally the case that large cattle, small cattle, and pigs are all slaughtered in one and the same slaughter-hall.

The small amount of slaughtering to be done allows of, and indeed almost demands, this economy of space. It is a fact established by long experience that a number of angles increases the cost of a building, and the same is true of a number of gables. The plan in question is therefore followed with a view to reducing expense.

In larger abattoirs for towns of more than 10,000 inhabitants, the slaughtering-halls for large and small cattle are generally combined in one; but in towns of more than 30,000 inhabitants the extent of slaughtering operations demands a separate hall for large and small animals. According as the block system or system of separate buildings is adopted, these halls will be under one roof, or independent of each other.

We may here allude to the fact that the old French

VIEW OF SMALL ABATTOIR, ROTHENBURG.
Slaughtering-hall for large and small animals.

system of separate slaughter-houses for each butcher has been long discarded. It is only in Holland, Switzerland, and Italy that old-fashioned abattoirs built on this plan are found.*

The old slaughter-house for large cattle at Buda Pesth is arranged in this way, but will shortly be replaced by a new building on thoroughly modern lines. The great

* We note with regret that the new abattoir in course of erection at Islington is of this old-fashioned type which Herr Heiss condemns.

defect of the French system is that it renders supervision much more difficult. It is, in fact, nothing but the old private slaughter-house system, the only difference being that the various isolated slaughter-houses are here collected under one roof. Such a system is precisely what the public abattoir is intended to obviate.

Quite recently there has been an entirely new departure in abattoir building, a combination of the block and separation system having been introduced. Covered

OFFENBACH ABATTOIR.

Covered roadway.

roadways are used, and by this means the separate buildings are combined into one.

The roadways are roofed with concrete vaulting, and have numerous skylights, so that sufficient light may find its way into the slaughtering-halls.

Premises built on these lines enable traffic to be carried on between different parts of the abattoir, regardless of wind or weather. Moreover, the long connecting passages, which were a necessary feature of the

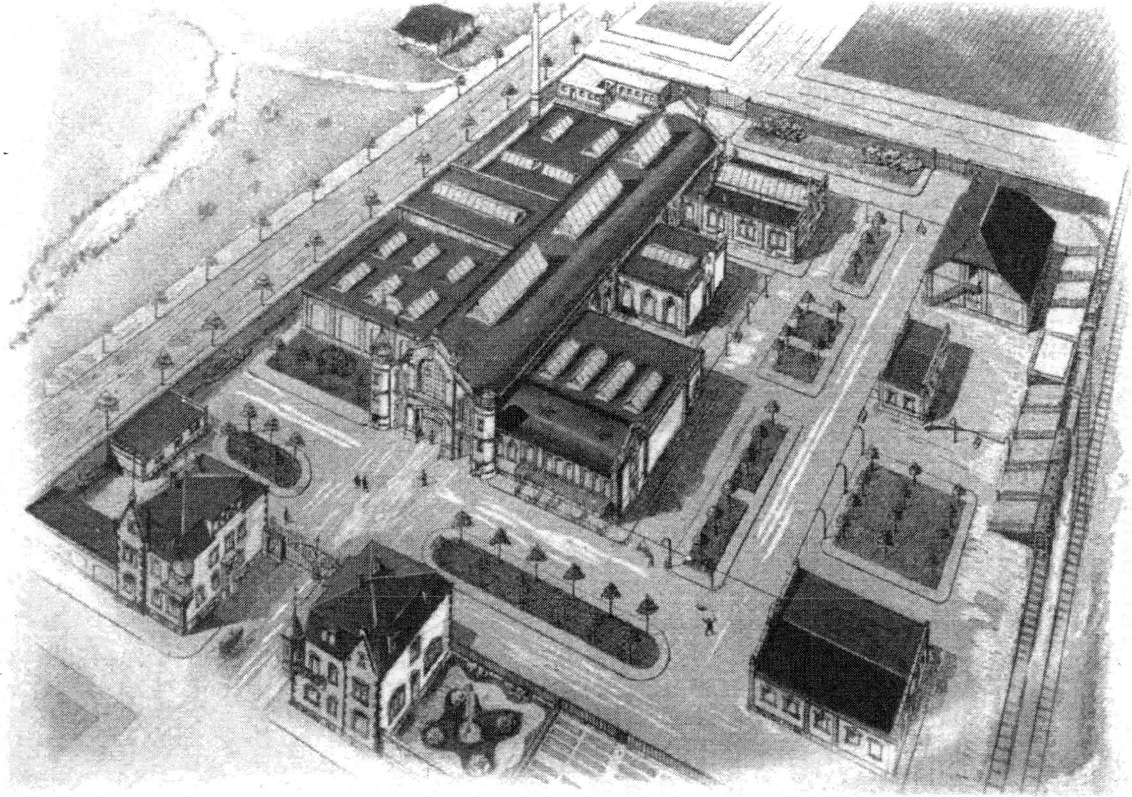

A SWISS ABATTOIR.

Fine abattoir at La Chaux de Fonds, Switzerland, mentioned by Herr Heiss.

original block system, are done away with, and along with them the cold draughts of air which were so trying to workers in the abattoir.

Excellent examples of the above system are to be found at La Chaux de Fonds in Switzerland, Mannheim, and Bamberg. We may also mention the abattoir in process of construction at Offenbach.

After having considered these purely structural points, it may be of interest to say a word as to the building and outfit of the most modern slaughtering-halls for all kinds of animals.

The magnificent examples of such slaughtering-halls to be found on the Continent are truly wonderful. We may cite as examples, St. Marx in Vienna, Augsburg, Bamberg, Mannheim, and Straubing.

Slaughtering-halls should not be less than 23 feet high. There are, indeed, halls which are 39 feet high, but this is excessive. On entering we find air and light in abundance. The daylight pours in through numerous large windows, with iron frames turning on pivots to admit the air.

As a rule, those windows which face the sun have frosted glass, so that the light may not dazzle the eyes of the workers. Besides the usual windows, some abattoirs have special fan-lights as well, as at Asch in Bohemia. The doors are generally made of corrugated iron. The flooring of a first-rate slaughter-hall should be of large granite slabs, laid so as to leave no interstices, or else of red sandstone.

A material which can be especially recommended for slaughter-halls is the red Weser sandstone, which has been widely used in America for a number of years. Broadway, New York, is an instance in point.

As a flooring for this particular purpose it is perfection, as the surface never wears smooth or into holes ;

OFFENBACH GREAT SLAUGHTERING-HALL.

its roughness is not too great, and it is capable of supporting heavy weights.

In many abattoirs light-coloured fire-clay flags, known as Saargemund or Mettlacher flags, are used, but practical experience shows that on the whole large slabs are preferable, since small flags work loose in course of time. Whatever material is used, no crevices must be left between the flags, but the joints must be filled in with cement. The use of asphalt has been discontinued on account of its slippery surface, and concrete is only employed from motives of economy.

At the same time, to attempt to save money in regard to the flooring which is exposed to the greatest amount of wear and tear is in the end false economy. A good floor only entails initial expenditure; an inferior one continual outlay for repairs. Above all, artificial tiles should be avoided, as nothing of this kind has stood the test of actual usage.

Slaughtering-halls, as a rule, consist of three longitudinal divisions, the two next the walls being used for slaughtering, the centre being the gangway for traffic.

The slope of the flooring is so arranged that the gutters run next to the walls, and the highest level is in the middle of the centre gangway. This, accordingly, always remains dry. The gutters are placed about 1 foot from the walls, must be of the requisite depth, and be provided with close-fitting gullies at every 3 yards or so, these gullies being the entrances to the drains. The gullies must be furnished with sand and grease-traps in order to, as far as possible, retain all solid matter in the waste-water. If good gullies are used, much of the work done by the sewage clarifying process will be saved.

The walls in slaughter-halls are always faced with some material which can be washed. In simply-built abattoirs this facing is of smooth cement, or of a coating

STRASSBURG ABATTOIR (SLAUGHTERING-HALL).

of waterproof enamel-colour laid on rough cement. The latter, however, requires to be renewed every two years, and is soon washed off.

We find slaughter-halls lined with glazed tiles, others faced with stone which can be washed; others even in which the walls are lined with large slabs of white marble—the most expensive, but at the same time the most perfect and durable, material. The abattoir at Straubing has this wall-facing.

Whatever material be used, the colour should not be dark, and the lighter it is the cleaner the walls will be kept by the butchers, and the cleaner the butchers themselves will be in their work generally. The best colour of all is pure white.

The wall-facing should rise to a height of from 5 to 10 feet from the floor. A white wall and a red floor go well together, and butchers will soon take a pride in smartly-kept slaughtering-halls, and see that when their work is over the whole place is, with the help of rubber 'squeegees,' made as clean as though it had never been used.

With regard to the ceilings of slaughter-halls, we find in old-fashioned establishments bare wooden beams. The style of ceiling has, however, long since been discarded, and been replaced by iron girders.

With the old-fashioned ceiling, with naked joists and timbers, ventilation was secured by means of louvre ventilators, which were objectionable because in winter it was impossible to close them. In hard winter, therefore, the cold in the slaughter-hall was severely felt. In consequence of this the old-fashioned ventilator has been completely superseded by modern mechanical contrivances, such as rotating ventilators.

In cold or stormy weather these ventilators can be closed by air-valves.

OVERHEAD TRANSPORT WITH SELF-LOCKING HOISTS.

The mechanical appliances forming the outfit of the slaughter-hall vary greatly, according to the different systems adopted. The old-fashioned crab-winch, worked by hand with hempen ropes and wooden gambrels, has long disappeared, having been replaced by iron self-locking hoists, with which the heaviest bullock can be easily raised with one hand. These hoists are so arranged that by reversing the handle the carcass can be lowered without any further action on the part of the butcher. If the handle is released, an automatic brake at once comes into play, and the carcass remains suspended at exactly the desired height.

In former days, when slaughter-houses were first constructed, it was not imagined that a system could be devised by which an animal's carcass could be at once removed from the place where it had been slaughtered, so as to leave both hoist and gambrel available for a second animal.

We have already mentioned that on this account the earlier abattoirs had to be much more extensive than those built at present, which, though of smaller dimensions, admit of the same amount of work being done.

The contrivance by which this is made possible is known as overhead transport. Its principle is as follows: Over every hoist are one or two T-shaped girders, on or between which run overhead travelling monkeys, forming a sort of aërial railway. The overhead runners, which are shown in the accompanying sketch, are used to remove carcasses attached to them to the hanging-house previous to entering the cold store.

The first arrangement of this kind was one with solid gambrels. The two halves of the split carcass hung at a distance of about 3 feet apart at the ends of the meat-tree, and had to be transferred along with the meat-tree to the overhead runners. Whenever, therefore, a fresh animal was slaughtered another meat-tree was required.

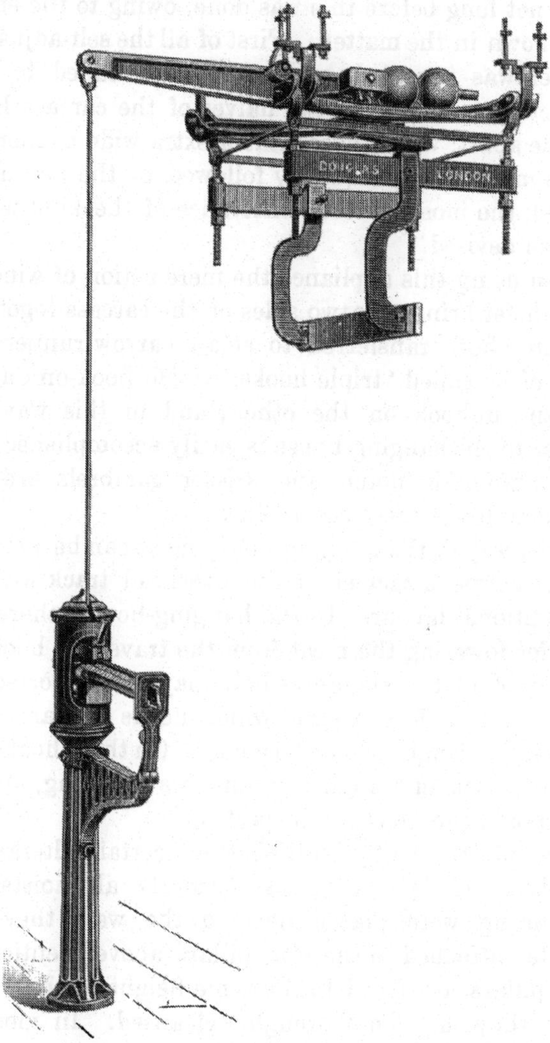

AUTOMATIC WEIGHING-MACHINE.

Taking down the carcass from an arrangement of this kind with solid gambrels was also attended with difficulties, so that an attempt was made to improve an apparatus which had already proved so practically useful. It was not long before this was done, owing to the enterprise shown in the matter. First of all the self-adjusting gambrel was invented, which, however, failed to give satisfaction because the two halves of the carcass hung too wide apart, which necessitated extra wide runners.

This invention was quickly followed by the automatic gambrel, the most perfect contrivance of the kind which has been devised.

When using this appliance the mere action of winding up the hoist brings the two sides of the carcass together. They are then transferred to small narrow runners by means of so-called 'triple hooks,' which hook on on one side, and unhook on the other; and in this way the removal to the hanging-house is easily accomplished.

The automatic notch and scissor gambrels are the best examples of these contrivances.

On the way to the hanging-house meat can be weighed on a machine attached to the overhead track without any additional labour. In the hanging-houses there are hoists for lowering the meat from the travelling hooks.

The roof of the slaughter-hall may be supported by massive iron pillars, around which hooks are arranged in circles at a height of 6 feet 6 inches. On these hooks the internal organs of slaughtered animals are hung, and in this position can be easily inspected.

In the most recently-built abattoirs certain alterations have been made. Whereas formerly all hoists for slaughtering were placed next to the wall, they are now often attached to the iron pillars above mentioned. These pillars are faced to the same height as the walls, so that they may be thoroughly cleansed. In modern abattoirs, indeed, cleanliness is carried to such a pitch that all corners are avoided, and the angle where wall and floor meet is rounded so that not a particle of dirt may be harboured.

In the slaughtering-hall, as well as in the other buildings of the abattoir, there are offices for the superintendents or hall-masters.

The slaughtering-rooms for calves, sheep, and goats, correspond, generally speaking, to those for large cattle, the only difference being that the overhead transport gear is absent.

In a few abattoirs there are overhead runners for carrying large calves to the cold store. Instead of hoists, hooks are used, to which the animals are hung after being stunned, to be skinned and cleaned.

The stunning is performed on slaughtering-trestles (killing-blocks), and the animal is bled immediately after. On account of the slope of the floor from the centre to the walls at the sides the hooks on the hook-frames, which are placed at right angles, are at different heights, varying from 6 feet to 6 feet 10 inches.

We may mention the fact that in all German abattoirs stunning before bleeding is strictly insisted on. In establishments which have an up-to-date equipment we find invariably a shooting apparatus of the latest design used for stunning. In establishments on a more modest scale iron clubs and hammers are used for the same purpose. The bouterolle, or 'slaughtering-mask,' which has long been known as a most satisfactory contrivance, has been very widely adopted, and may be recommended on the ground of being inexpensive to keep in repair.

Animals are Never Slaughtered without Being Stunned.

It is felt that an animal's death should be made as painless as possible, and our societies for the prevention of cruelty to animals—which are to be found in every town—make a point of urging the principle of humane slaughtering. With this object they supply the abattoirs with the latest stunning appliances, and contribute regularly to defray the cost of ammunition.

Employment of Modern Appliances for Stunning Cattle.

(The following description of various humane slaughtering appliances employed in Germany is here reprinted from Herr Heiss's essay on humane slaughtering.)

The slaughtering-mask, or bouterolle, the first real improvement in modern methods of slaughtering, is no longer a novelty.

It has been adopted in most German abattoirs, and also in many private slaughter-houses.

The construction of this apparatus is obvious from the diagram on opposite page. As to the way in which the bouterolle is to be fixed on the animal its very construction will prevent any mistake being made.

Care must only be taken to prevent its slipping to one side, since this would involve injury to only one side of the brain. The bolt penetrates into the skull at an angle almost, therefore, in the direction of the spinal cord. If the bolt be driven by a blow with the iron-bound mallet from four to five inches into the brain, it will penetrate between the two halves of the brain, carrying with it a disc of bone which it punches out (or its splintered fragments), shatter the surface of the brain, and rupture numerous bloodvessels. The stricken animal collapses instantly.

In order to preserve the cutting power of the bolt it should never be dropped on the floor, which would blunt the cutting-edge. The bolt should be cleaned every time it is used as hair and fragments of bone may clog the sharpened end and lessen its cutting power. Now and then, also, the groove in the metal plate should be greased.

The wooden mallet should have both faces perfectly flat, and without holes, which might cause it to slip off the head of the bolt. The striking-bolt apparatus has been employed for smaller cattle in many abattoirs with remarkable success.

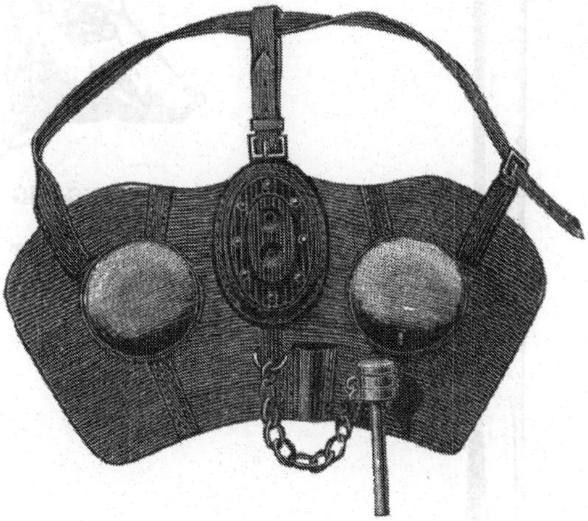

BANNEAU MASK.

Calves and sheep allow the bolt to be applied to the forehead without difficulty. One slaughterman holds the bolt in the proper place—with calves, in the middle of the forehead; with sheep, at the apex of the skull, almost between the ears—and a second assistant strikes the head of the bolt with the mallet, which drives it into the skull and produces immediate insensibility.

In the case of pigs, the Kleinschmidt hammer with spring-bolt, and the lever-bolt hammer made by Blumhaus, of Vohwinkel, have proved most satisfactory. If the bolt be placed a finger's breadth above the eyes in the centre of the skull a steady stroke will drive it into the

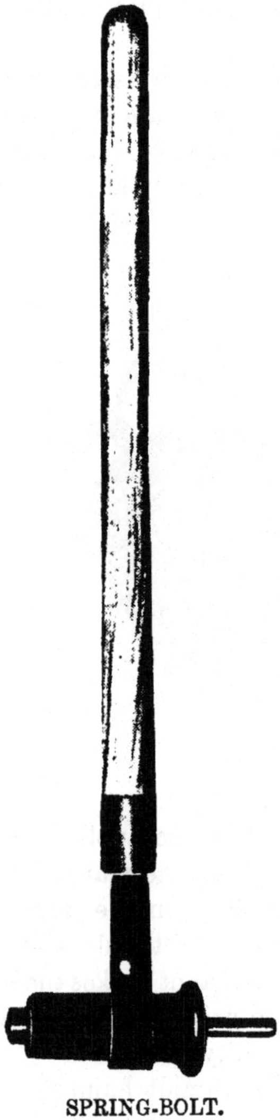

SPRING-BOLT.

STUNNING PIG WITH KLEINSCHMIDT SPRING-BOLT.

STUNNING SHEEP WITH STRIKING-BOLT.

brain and cause the animal to collapse without a sound. Occasionally the animal remains standing after being stunned, with its legs spread out trestlewise, and has to be pushed over. A pressure on the lever easily withdraws the bolt from the skull, and the apparatus is then ready for further use. Avoid applying the hammer to a spot too high up on the skull, as in that case the bolt will only pierce the large frontal cavity, causing pain but not stunning the animal.

The Kleinschmidt spring-bolt, which has given most satisfactory results in hundreds of slaughtering establishments, consists of an iron cylinder, in which a gouge-shaped bolt is fitted, surrounded by a strong spiral spring. The cylinder is attached to a handle. The bolt is applied to the animal's skull, and driven into the brain by a blow with a mallet. The spring is compressed by the blow, and its recoil withdraws the bolt from the brain.

This apparatus is manufactured by Schumann and Kuchler of Erfurt, as well as by Renger of Annstadt. Kogler of Chemnitz has constructed a 'slot-hole bolt apparatus'; the bolt, however, is not withdrawn mechanically. Kurten of Barmen has contrived a spring-bolt apparatus, in which the bolt's line of movement is intersected at right angles by two long springs. These springs are driven together by the blow which drives in the bolt, and as they naturally tend to fly apart again they thus release the bolt. The apparatus manufactured by Blumhaus of Vohwinkel, mentioned above, also belongs to this group. Any of these appliances are suitable for slaughtering calves. The Kurten apparatus is excellent for sheep, but the Kleinschmidt swage with fixed bolt may also be used with advantage.

Shooting Apparatus.

With Bullet.

A great advance in slaughtering was made by the invention of the shooting apparatus. The first appliance of this kind was so constructed that instead of the groove for a bolt a pistol-barrel was fixed in the slaughtering-mask. The discharge was effected by an igniting apparatus at the base of the barrel. The shooting apparatus now made—the best of which are manufactured by Messrs. Stoff of Erfurt—work so quietly through noiseless powder being used that no objection can be made on the score of their noise interfering with slaughter-house work. In those forms of apparatus in particular which are provided with several silencing chambers the report is so wonderfully deadened that the sound resembles that made by a person clapping his hands.

With regard to the employment of the shooting apparatus with bullets we should like to add a few words.

All fire-arms, whether guns or pistols, may, as we know, be considered dangerous. Now, the shooting apparatus is simply a modified pistol. When once the breech is closed, there is no guarantee that it may not explode. The only safe method is not to screw up the butt completely until standing in front of the animal to be killed.

Careless handling of the shooting apparatus may therefore endanger the lives of bystanders.

It is true that we may point to long experience in the use of the apparatus. It is true that when carefully handled it is not dangerous. At the same time there are on record cases of accidents—even fatal accidents—occasioned by the apparatus in question. It would, however, be wrong to summarily reject this kind of slaughter appliances on these grounds, since in most cases careless handling has been to blame.

The danger of the contrivance lies in the uncontrolled course of the bullet after leaving the barrel. The great mistake generally made is that when dealing with large cattle, which requires a heavy charge of powder to kill—that is, to give the requisite penetrative power—the shot

SLAUGHTERING BULLOCK WITH SHOOTING APPARATUS.

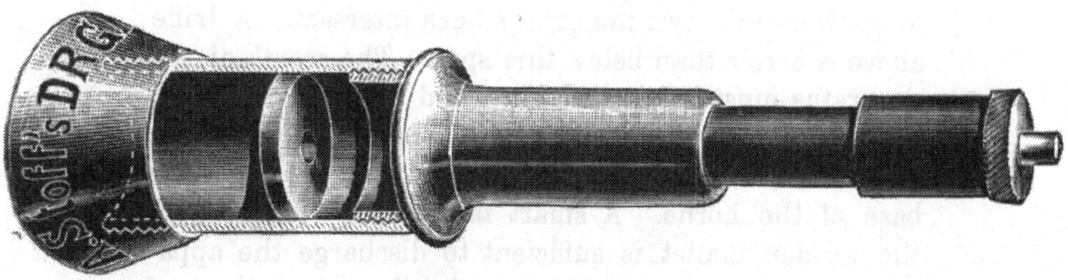

STOFF'S SHOOTING APPARATUS.

is carelessly fired, the direction which the bullet will take not being sufficiently noted. The bullet, when it leaves the barrel, will, unless it be deflected by some unforeseen obstacle, pursue a straight course, and this will carry it through the brain into the cervical vertebræ, where it is generally found. If the animal's head is turned sideways, and therefore is not in a direct line with the spine, the bullet may reappear at one side of the neck, and may even pierce the skin, which generally happens when a large charge of powder is used. That under certain circumstances the bullet may thus injure bystanders, is of course, quite possible.

Care should, therefore, be taken to keep neck and head in one straight line, and also for the additional reason that if the flesh of the neck is pierced injuries are done and bleeding caused.

Above all, let nobody stand in front of the person who is firing.

It is very rarely necessary to hold the animal, as a bullock's forehead offers a broad surface, and the spot where the shot should strike is so clearly indicated that a miss is hardly possible. If we look at the diagram on the previous page, we shall see exactly how the right spot may be found.

Let a line be drawn from each eye to the base of the horn on the opposite side. The correct spot will be found where the two imaginary lines intersect. A trifle above is better than below this spot. The *mouth* of the apparatus must be applied here, and not the *upper rim*. We may also take a line for the brain by placing the mouth of the apparatus four fingers' breadth below the base of the horns. A smart tap on the plunger with the wooden mallet is sufficient to discharge the apparatus. Avoid using a brightly-painted mallet, or one of a red colour, unless the animal is wearing a mask. Many animals dislike bright colours, especially horses.

In dealing with the latter animal some practice is required in the use of the shooting apparatus. Horses shot too high in the head generally fall over, while those shot too low spring forwards and upwards. The operator must therefore feel with his fingers, so as to accurately locate the spot where the two bony ridges—of which we have already spoken—merge into one. This is the spot to which the mouth of the apparatus must be applied.

Shooting appliances for small cattle have also been

SLAUGHTERING PIG WITH BULLET.

devised, and pigs and sheep are slaughtered with them in many abattoirs. With sheep the same rule applies for shooting as for felling, and the point aimed at should be the apex of the skull. With pigs, too, the spot for either blow or shot is identical. Sheep offer no resistance, but a certain amount of practice is necessary in handling pigs. The operator posts himself to the left of the head, places the apparatus deliberately on the centre of the skull, and, avoiding all haste, as soon as the animal is quiet, strikes the bolt.

The advantages of the shooting apparatus must be obvious to everyone, whether he be a slaughterman or not. The instantaneous result will cause all the more astonishment, because the puniest man is able to kill large bulls with perfect ease.

There are certain disadvantages, however, connected with every contrivance, and here we are not thinking of the various accidents referred to above. In slaughtering with the bouterolle, nothing is left in the animal's body after the bolt has been withdrawn. We merely see a small hole, from which the blood trickles.

When a shot is fired, the case is different. The opening made is, indeed, smaller than that produced by the bolt, but it can be easily understood how impossible it is to prevent explosive gases making their way into the brain after the bullet. They, of course, constitute the projective force. There is, therefore, a possibility that the brain may thus acquire a gaseous smell.

A second point to remember is that, when once fired the bullet travels unchecked through the body. When its initial impetus is exhausted, it will bury itself in some part of the head or neck, either in flesh or bone. If the shot has been fired according to the directions given—that is to say, with the neck held straight—it will generally be found in the first cervical vertebra, and will fall out when the carcass is split.

Contact with any hard object—in this case bone—will cause it to lose its original shape more or less. When found in the spot mentioned above, it can do no further mischief.

The case is, however, different if the bullet pierces the spinal column sideways, and is lost in the flesh of the neck. Even here it is often found again when the flesh is stripped from the bones of a bull to be worked up into sausages—that is to say, if the slaughterman takes a little trouble about it. Often, however, in spite of his efforts, it cannot be found. In the case of bullocks and cows this is immaterial. In the case of bulls, however, unpleasant consequences for the butcher are apt to ensue, since when the pieces of meat containing the bullet are thrown into the sausage-machine, they will pass through the machine, until suddenly the hidden bullet will break off one or more knives. This is especially likely to happen if the bullet is capped with steel to increase its penetration; whereas when bullets made of so-called leadless compositions are found, they are cut up into discs and tiny sections.

The curious noise made by the machine will at once inform us if this has happened. In this case the meat is discoloured by fragments of metal or tin, and has to be thrown away.

Such unpleasant occurrences are of little importance, however, while the advantage of not shattering the animal's skull, but only making a small hole in it, outweighs other considerations. *When the bullet is used, however, caution is always needed.* We shall now see how, to avoid the disadvantages belonging to this kind of apparatus, the attempt was made to use powder in driving a bolt into the animal's brain instead of a bullet.

The Shooting-bolt Apparatus.

Just as shooting was intended to be, and indeed was, an improvement on the striking-bolt, so the shooting-bolt apparatus is a material advance on shooting with the bullet. It absolutely prevents the uncontrolled flight of a projectile which may cause mischief; it prevents explosive gases penetrating into the brain; it makes it impossible for bystanders to be injured by stray bullets: in short, it obviates all the drawbacks attaching to the use of the bullet.

These reasons alone constitute advantages on the part of the shooting-bolt apparatus which are not to be underrated. The fundamental idea of the apparatus is as follows: The bolt which was originally driven into the brain of the animal by physical force, whose action cannot be depended upon, is now propelled by an absolutely reliable agent—gunpowder. By exploding a small cartridge with a mallet, the bolt is driven forward with the speed of lightning from its resting-place inside the apparatus, and penetrates into the animal's brain.

The principle on which the apparatus is constructed is as follows: A bolt, similar to those with which we are now familiar as used in the striking-bolt apparatus, is fitted in a strongly-made cylinder, with a bore of about 3 centimetres, closed at its lower end with a plate. This plate has an opening in the centre about 1 centimetre wide. The head of the bolt is thicker than the rest, and works to and fro inside the cylinder. Behind the head of the bolt lies the cartridge-chamber. The cartridge is inserted with a slight pressure of the finger, and the breech is closed by turning the lever sideways. The apparatus is then ready to fire. The charge is exploded by a tap with the mallet, and the bolt driven like lightning into the brain.

The management of the apparatus does not differ materially from that of the shooting apparatus except in this point, that in employing the latter the operator remains standing after the shot has been fired, whereas with this kind of shooting-bolt apparatus he must stoop down as the animal falls, since the bolt is firmly fixed in the skull, and can only be released by a vigorous wrench.

Quite recently a new apparatus has excited a good

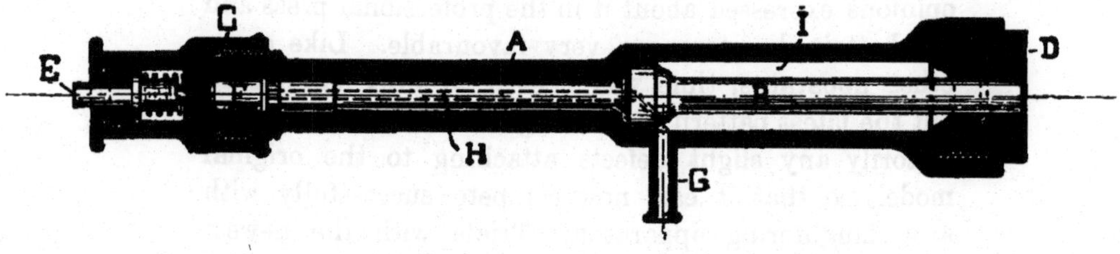

SHOOTING-BOLT APPARATUS (ORIGINAL PATTERN).

A. Barrel.
B. Bolt.
C. Breech.
D. Muzzle.
E. Plunger.
F. Cartridge.
G. Vent for gas to escape.
H. Explosive gas.
I. Cylinder containing bolt.

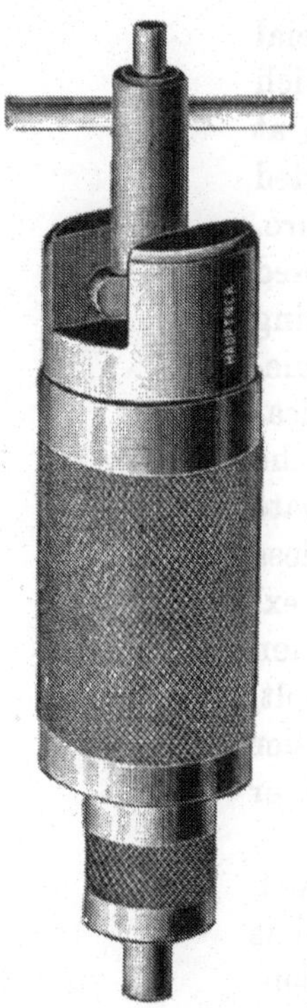

FLESSA APPARATUS.

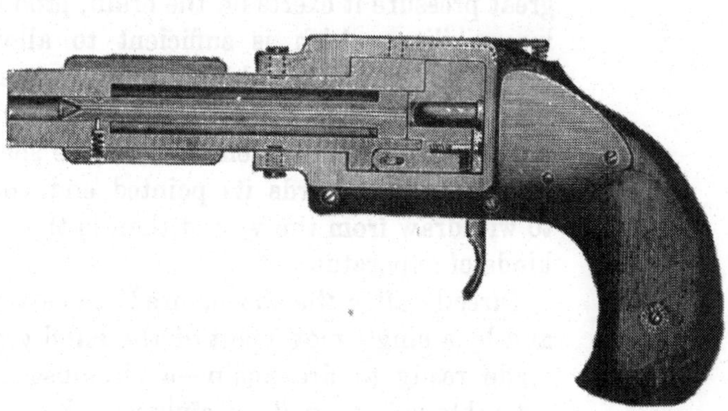

BEHR'S 'FLASH CATTLE-KILLER.'

deal of attention—Behr's 'Flash Cattle-killer.' The opinions expressed about it in the professional press and by abattoir directors are very favourable. Like every other apparatus, time was needed to fully develop it, but the latest pattern has managed to obviate most satisfactorily any slight defects attaching to the original model, so that it can now compete successfully with any slaughtering apparatus. Trials with the newest pattern have shown it to be eminently practical.

The construction of the apparatus is that of a breech-loading ejector pistol. The barrel contains a special kind of conical-shaped bolt, through the core of which a hole is drilled, terminating in two small openings at the sides of the pointed ends; the cartridge is inserted in the breech, which is easily closed by lateral pressure. The apparatus, being now ready to fire, is pressed against the animal's forehead, and discharged by pulling the trigger, the bolt piercing the skull-bone and penetrating into the cranial cavity. Not only the mechanical action of the bolt, but also the irruption of gas and the great pressure it exerts on the brain, produces immediate insensibility, which is sufficient to allow of painless bleeding. The bolt, which is shot forward by the explosion, is driven back almost into its original position by an ingenious arrangement, and the shape of the bolt, which tapers towards its pointed end, renders it easier to withdraw from the wound than is the case with other kinds of apparatus.

Directly after the shot is fired the cartridge is ejected, and by a single movement of the hand the apparatus is made ready to fire again—a circumstance which considerably enhances its usefulness when slaughtering is done on a large scale.

Another advantage possessed by the apparatus, which is not to be underrated, is that it can be employed the whole day without being cleaned. Care must only be taken to see that the openings for the gas to escape are not choked with splinters of bone. This, however, can be done with very little trouble. The particular kind of powder employed is such that the brain acquires no kind of taste from it.

A point which is of importance as concerning its general utility is that the same apparatus can be used for small and large cattle, the strength of the charge alone being altered.

Quite recently, with a view to increasing the penetration of the bolt, Behr has reverted to the reliable old circular cutting-edge, similar to what we find used with the ordinary slaughtering-mask. The bolt contains a passage for the gas, so that when the shot is fired the gas forces its way through the bolt into the brain. This arrangement renders the pistol somewhat shorter and thicker, and therefore handier to use. The return of the bolt has been also materially improved. In addition to this, the inventor has added a new and practical contrivance in the shape of a muzzle-rest with foot-plate, which makes it possible to use the same apparatus for all kinds of cattle, since the rest prevents the bolt penetrating too deeply when used with small animals. The plate also makes it easier to hold the apparatus steady.

In its present form this apparatus will doubtless be very popular, and all the more so because its workmanship may be described as first-rate.

Slaughtering-Hall for Pigs.

A further insight into the internal arrangements of the abattoir is obtained by visiting the slaughter-hall for pigs.

In constructing this building regard must be had to

the necessary distinction between the sticking and scalding room and the room for cutting-up proper. The reason for this division lies in the fact that in dealing with pigs the work is divided into two processes: (1) Killing and scalding; (2) cutting-up.

Close to the killing and scalding rooms resting-pens are usually built, leading from the styes in which the animals waiting to be killed are kept. Similar pens are also used for small animals, being built adjoining the stalls for such animals. The fasting-pens are surrounded by iron gratings, and the passages leading from one to another are closed by doors with an automatic fastening. By a special arrangement the doors of a pen can be opened from either side. If it is desired to drive pigs from one pen into another the door is opened in such a way as to shut off part of the passage until the pigs have been driven into another pen; the door is then closed, and opened on the other side, so that pigs can be driven into the pen which has just been cleared.

Passages lead from the resting-pens into the killing and scalding room. The animals are first stunned with a club or some other instrument, and then stuck while lying on the floor, the blood used for making sausages being caught in shallow pans.

Heavy animals are lifted by a swinging crane with safety-windlass into the scalding-vat which stands ready, and when the bristles have been removed are again lifted on to one of the scuttling-tables to be thoroughly cleaned.

In better-arranged abattoirs the walls and floors of the sticking-pens, which were formerly merely of concrete, are covered with white tiles. By this means the work of sticking is made more cleanly, because with a hose all blood can be at once washed down the trapped drain in the middle of the sticking-pen.

FRANKFORT ABATTOIR.

Slaughtering-hall for pigs, with scalding-vats.

Over the scuttling-tables there are rubber hose with copper rose-heads, so that the carcasses can be thoroughly rinsed with water after the hair has been removed. Not until this has been done are they transferred to the disembowelling-bar to be hung up and cleaned.

The work of hanging up the carcasses is facilitated by the overhead transport arrangement. The pigs are raised from the scuttling-tables by pulleys, then attached to the overhead runners, and so conveyed to any hook to which they are to be hung. No special exertion is required on the part of the slaughterman.

With regard to the hooks, their arrangement closely resembles that in the slaughter-hall for small animals.

After the carcasses have been dressed they are examined by the meat inspector, but samples of the flesh must first be examined for 'trichinæ.' This has to be done by a specially-appointed 'trichinosis' inspector. If the meat is passed as sound, it is then stamped and handed over as fit for sale.

In old-fashioned abattoirs carcasses had usually to be carried to the hanging-houses of the cold store, after passing the meat inspector. A recent invention has, however, quite done away with the fixed hook-frames.

In well-arranged abattoirs the scalding-room is divided from the cutting-up room by a partition made of plaster or glass, which reaches from the ceiling to within about 3 yards of the floor. The steam rising from the scalding-vats is carried off through large ventilators fixed in the roof of the scalding-room, which is generally vaulted. By this means the steam causes no inconvenience.

The Tripe-House.

The fittings of the tripe-house require especial attention, because the very nature of the work carried on there necessitates the presence of dirt. The refuse scraped

HILDESHEIM ABATTOIR.

Scalding-vats and crane.

from animals' stomachs, the hair from the feet and muzzles of bullocks, are strewed on the floor. The contents of the smaller intestines is collected in special receptacles and carried away to the manure-house. The tripe-house should contain at least two scalding-vats, even in the smallest abattoirs—one for scalding the feet and heads of animals, the other for cleansing the intestines. Besides this there should be basins with so-called 'steam-heaters,' provided for supplementary purposes, as, for instance, cleaning the feet before they are scalded.

Washing-troughs of enamel or earthenware for cleaning the entrails and intestines of small animals are placed along the walls. They are arranged in pairs, and between every two pairs there are tripe-scraping tables of oak, with an iron flange for removing fat from the intestines.

The washing-troughs have a supply of hot and cold water, and by the use of steam-heaters the desired temperature can be obtained. Clean chopping-blocks are provided, on which the muzzles of animals are cut off, so as to save the flooring of the tripe-house. In many cases the offal-house is found directly adjoining the slaughter-hall for large or small cattle or that for pigs. In large establishments, however, the building is isolated, so as to prevent unpleasant smells penetrating into the slaughter-halls. Frequently the offal-house is in direct communication with the manure-house.

The Manure-House.

The manure-house is where the contents of the stomach and intestines are emptied out before these parts are further dealt with. The intestines are carried to the manure-house on hand-carts, and there deposited on the floor and emptied. The manure collected in this way is dropped through a shoot in the flooring into manure-carts standing below. When these are full, an

TRIPERY (ZERBST ABATTOIR).
Showing washing-troughs, scuttling-table, etc.

air-tight covering is screwed down and they are driven away. Manure-houses are generally so arranged that the carts do not have to pass through the abattoir yard, but go direct through a special gateway used for this purpose. In the case of large abattoirs, instead of carts drawn by horses, specially constructed railway trucks are used, and a branch siding is built for them.

As to the appointments of the manure-house, some buildings are of the simplest description, and others are fitted up so as to be kept admirably clean—*e.g.*, the manure-house in the abattoir at Bamberg, where the walls are faced with slabs, and even the shoots are lined with tiles.

The rinsing-troughs placed in the manure-house are generally of enamel or concrete, and are used for the preliminary washing of the internal organs before they are passed on to the tripe-house.

N.B.—*The best way to encourage cleanliness is to have places where dirty work has to be done smartly fitted up.*

The Lairage.

Even if a cattle-market is not combined with the abattoir, an arrangement which, as we have said, would not pay in smaller towns, there must be lairage for cattle which have been driven or brought to the abattoir, and are waiting to be killed. The lairage must be sufficiently roomy to accommodate the largest number of animals likely to be brought to the abattoir, so as to prevent cattle being housed inside the town, as was formerly the case.

To secure this being done, the lowest possible fee should be exacted for the use of the lairage, and animals should be allowed to remain there for twenty-four hours free of charge. Fodder, etc., should be sold at such a price as to merely cover the cost. A small charge is generally made at so much a head per day for attending to cattle, and, as a rule, willingly paid.

With regard to the appointments of the lairage, there should be nothing luxurious, but the first and most essential point to bear in mind is facility for disinfecting. The material used for the building must not be liable to suffer from the unavoidable use of chemical disinfectants. Stone and iron may be used, but *wood never*. The walls, up to a height of over 6 feet, must be of impervious material which can be washed. This must also be the case with the fodder-racks and flooring. With regard to doors, the latest idea is to have them of corrugated iron.

We need not mention that the lairage, like the other premises, must be kept scrupulously clean by the abattoir staff.

It is advisable, where there is no cattle-market, to have the landing-platform for cattle which have arrived by rail close to the lairage, so that the animals have not far to go to the abattoir. This prevents the spread of infection in case of an epidemic. Landing-platforms should be built of stone and iron. Permeable macadam is most objectionable. It must be possible to remove all animal excrement with perfect cleanliness. There should always be a supply of water at such platforms for watering thirsty cattle, and also hose for sluicing pigs, which stand much in need of this after a long railway journey in hot weather.

In many abattoirs the landing-platform and sanitary establishment for diseased cattle are in connection. Until animals have been found free from infectious disease nothing further may be done with them.

The departments of the abattoir which we have at present described are absolutely essential, even in the smallest establishments. The *modern* abattoir, however, includes a number of supplementary sections which, while not being exactly indispensable, are yet most desirable on sanitary grounds. The most important of such accessory buildings is the slaughter-house for diseased cattle.

Live animals which show symptoms of disease may not be brought into the public slaughtering-hall to be killed, but must be taken to the sanitary slaughter-house especially reserved for diseased animals. Animals which while alive show no signs of being diseased, but which when slaughtered prove to be so, must be removed to the sanitary slaughter-house for the carcasses to be further dealt with and for certain sanitary measures to be taken. It would be a mistake to consider that this building may be fitted up in the roughest fashion. On the contrary, it is precisely premises of this kind which, from their somewhat abnormal character, enjoy less consideration, which should have their status raised by the excellence of their appointments. Above all, such buildings must be easy to disinfect thoroughly.

Special mechanical appliances, such as overhead track-bars, etc., may be dispensed with. It is usual to connect the lairage for diseased cattle with the sanitary slaughter-house; and this is advisable, because, in case of an epidemic breaking out among cattle in the town, they can be perfectly isolated here with a view to checking the spread of the disease.

Sterilising-Room.

Adjoining the sanitary slaughter-house is a special room, in which a sterilising apparatus is set up. This appliance, by means of a steam bath, converts meat which in a raw state is permeated with disease germs into a wholesome article of diet. It is obvious that in this way thousands of pounds' worth of meat may be utilised which would otherwise be wasted.

THE 'FREIBANK,' OR CERTIFIED COOKED MEAT SHOP.

The 'Freibank,' or 'Sanitäts-bank,' is an institution within the abattoir premises, where meat of an inferior quality is sold. Under no conditions is the flesh

ADMINISTRATIVE BLOCK.

LAIRAGE AND FREIBANK.

GERMAN ABATTOIR, ROTHENBURG.

of animals which have died of disease allowed to be offered for public sale, nor may whole carcasses of such animals be removed from the abattoir. The 'Freibank' often adjoins the sterilising-room, and, as a rule, there is a special entrance from the outside to the sale-room, so that purchasers at the 'Freibank' need not pass through the abattoir itself. As to the appointments of the 'Freibank,' what has been said of the sanitary establishment is doubly true here.

In many abattoirs the sale-room for inferior meat is a model of perfection, the object being to excite the emulation of local meat-dealers, who would not wish their establishments to compare unfavourably with the 'Freibank,' where inferior meat is sold. An admirable example of a model 'Freibank' is to be found in the abattoir at Bamberg. The walls are faced with white tiles right up to the ceiling, and the flooring and counters covered with the same material. The weighing-machines are nickel-plated and have marble slabs for scales, also mounted in nickel, which gives a smart appearance. There is a special entrance and exit for those entering and leaving the 'Freibank.' The waiting-room has a warming apparatus, and there are forms to sit on.

Condemned-Meat Room.

In all recently-erected abattoirs there is a room in the sanitary establishment in which the carcasses of diseased animals can be kept till they are further dealt with, without their being a source of annoyance or danger.

These rooms are lighted with hollow glass bricks, the walls are faced with material easy to disinfect, and the doors can be closed hermetically, so that not even flies—the plague of every abattoir—can find their way in.

In such rooms iron cylinders, which can also be hermetically closed, are used for the safe keeping of tuberculous or other dangerous diseased flesh. By means of a connection with the steam conduit it is possible to render the contents of these cylinders perfectly innocuous by sterilisation.

The Laboratory.

Adjoining the sanitary department we find, even in the least elaborate abattoir, a handsomely-fitted laboratory for the use of veterinary surgeons. Microscopes of the best make, germ-beds for the culture of bacteria, every kind of apparatus for examining milk, meat, or food, is abundantly supplied. There are also lavatories with hot and cold water, where the operator may cleanse and disinfect his hands; and stored in dainty cases are carefully-prepared examples of interesting malformations or abnormal growths which have been met with in the course of investigation. Such a laboratory gives the veterinary surgeon opportunities for original research, and especially for verifying diagnoses which have been made.

Dressing-Rooms.

In building an abattoir a dressing-room for those who habitually use the institution should not be forgotten. This is a great aid to cleanliness, since it enables butchers and their assistants to come to the abattoir in clean clothes. These can then be exchanged for their working-dress, kept in lockers in the dressing-room; and when work is over the men can resume their ordinary clothes before leaving the premises. There should be wash-hand basins in the dressing-room which are emptied by tilting, and butchers will gladly avail themselves of this convenience. In many abattoirs shower-baths, or even warm hip-baths, are attached to the dressing-room, and their use is allowed once a week free of charge. Bath-rooms of all kinds, simple or luxurious, are found in different abattoirs. One of the best examples of the kind is the bath-room in the abattoir at Plauen.

Engine and Boiler Houses.

If an abattoir has no cold store it requires no engine-house.

The hot water used in slaughter-house work, and also the steam required for heating the scalding-vats, can be supplied simply from a boiler house. The case is, of course, different if the abattoir has to generate its own electric light. A small steam-engine must in that case be installed to work the dynamo, and a larger engine if the water used in the abattoir is pumped up on the spot. If, however, we assume that a cold-store is attached to the abattoir, such a store will require its own engine and boiler house, and a special room for the refrigerating machinery.

The dimensions of this room will depend on the size of the cold store.

The Cold Store.

In Germany the addition of a cold store to the abattoir has become a *sine qua non*. No modern abattoir worthy of the name is without one; and this is not only true of large establishments, but also of moderate-sized and small ones, in which this useful adjunct is well represented. Klingenberg, for instance, a little town of 1,200 inhabitants, has an admirable abattoir *with* cold store and electric lighting plant. Most superb specimens of the cold store are to be found in the abattoirs of Berlin, Cologne, Frankfort, Mainz, Buda-Pesth, Linz, and Bamberg.

It has often been observed that when an abattoir has been built without a cold store it is not long before one is added, in compliance with the general wish. In fact, it is not merely the butcher who is aware of the value of a cold store. The general public also fully appreciate

ENTRANCE TO COLD STORE, OFFENBACH.

STORAGE CELLS IN COLD STORE.

the improved flavour of meat which has been kept and matured in this superior manner.

To the butcher, of course, the cold store is of benefit, because it enables him to take advantage of every turn of the market—to buy when cattle are cheap and to sell when meat is dear. Moreover, he can always keep a reserve of meat for emergencies without having to fear that one particle of it will undergo the process of decomposition. Again, the cold store will save him the yearly recurring expense of stocking and keeping up an ice-cellar. Even with such an ice-cellar he will lose large quantities of meat in the course of a year. What he saves in this respect alone will cover the rent of his safe at the cold store.

The cold store, indeed, reconciles the butcher to compulsory public slaughter. Its value is proved by the fact that large meat-dealers have their own private store. It must be remembered, however, that a public cold store is far more cheaply managed than a private one. There is saving in the case of the former both of material and labour.

We need insist no further on the advantages of cold storage, since the system has been fully tested in England. Great use of the invention was first made there in the way of importing frozen meat from other countries. Anyone who has seen the frozen-meat ships and storage accommodation at the London Docks will need no further proof that the English public is alive to the value of this method of preserving meat. We are here, of course, speaking of frozen meat, but from *freezing* to *chilling* meat is no great step to take. In a meat-freezing establishment the meat can be kept fresh for an almost unlimited time. In an abattoir cold store, on the other hand, the temperature is not below freezing-point, nor does meat, when removed from the store, require to be thawed. The temperature is generally from 2° to 8° above freezing, and the air kept dry by machinery enables meat to be kept in a perfect state of preservation for several months.

The architectural structure of the modern cold store is a matter deserving attention. Originally it was con-

INTERIOR OF COLD STORE.

sidered of vital importance that the walls should be of great thickness, so as to allow of a hollow space filled with air or some non-conducting substance. At the present day, however, the walls of the cold store are no thicker than those of the other buildings of the abattoir, but are covered by a non-conducting lining of cork. Underground cold stores are to be avoided as far as possible.

Admirable examples of the latest pattern of cold store, and well worth visiting, are the premises for storing all kinds of provisions belonging to the Trading and Cold-Storage Company at Leipzig, Berlin, and Vienna.

The cold store of an abattoir must be fitted up in such a way as to be kept scrupulously clean, both on account of preserving the meat which is stored there and also because, in view of the necessity of keeping the air dry, the lavish use of water must be prohibited.

A fact which has often been proved by experience is that a cold store is always kept cleaner by the butchers the more its appointments incite to cleanliness. White is the colour chosen for cold stores of the latest design. A special reason for preferring this colour is that it helps to light up the interior of the store.

The original idea was that no daylight should be admitted into the store, and some stores were even built lighted only by electricity. Nowadays, however, the opinion has gained ground that a store may be exposed to full daylight by means of windows and skylights without the slightest detriment; in fact, daylight and white colouring are two points specially insisted on in modern cold store.

The interior of the store itself is divided up into compartments enclosed with round iron bars, which the butchers rent at an average price of from thirty to fifty shillings a year for every 10 square feet of space.

The compartments are covered with white enamel paint, and the flooring is generally of buff-coloured tiles.

The appearance of a modern cold store with all the latest improvements is very pleasing, much more so than the dark old-fashioned type, with drab-coloured walls. The sight of such an establishment makes the public realise the superiority of the modern cold store as compared with the wooden structures formerly in vogue as cold stores or ice-houses.

The proper size of the cold store has been differently computed. Osthoff, taking as his basis the average amount of meat consumed per head in the course of a year—namely, 150 pounds—and the requisite space for every individual inhabitant—namely, $\frac{1}{12}$ square foot—arrives at a space of 10 square feet for every 120 inhabitants.

Schmitz, Linde, Stetefeld, and Dr. Schwarz, on the other hand, start with a different principle—namely, the storage capacity of the individual cold cells. These well-known authorities are agreed that 330 pounds of meat can be stored in every 10 square feet. Supposing, therefore, that in a town of 20,000 inhabitants there are annually slaughtered 1,860 large cattle, 5,380 small cattle, and 6,840 pigs, then on any of two principal slaughtering days per week 18·6 large cattle, 53·8 small animals, and 68·4 pigs are slaughtered. If we take the average weight of cattle, as established by statistics—namely, for large cattle, 603 pounds; for calves, 82 pounds; for sheep, 48 pounds; and for pigs, 180 pounds—we get 18·6 × 603 pounds = 11,216 pounds; + 53·8 × 65 pounds = 3,497 pounds; + 68·4 × 180 = 12,312 pounds; total, 27,102 pounds of meat, which must be stored at one and the same time in the cold store. Besides this, we have to take into consideration a quarter of the amount stated—that is to say, 6,775½ pounds, which has remained over from the preceding slaughtering day. Altogether, therefore, the total will reach 33,877 pounds.

If, therefore, as we have stated, 330 pounds of meat

can be stored on 10 square feet of space, then 10 square feet multiplied by 103 (that being the quotient, roughly speaking, of 33,877 divided by 330) will be the amount of storage-room required.

It is generally calculated that the gangways in a cold store should be 4 feet 10 inches wide. We must therefore add 310 square feet to the storage-room of 1,030 square feet, or about one-third of the whole floor-space; so that for a town of 20,000 inhabitants the interior of the cold store must measure 1,340 square feet.

The size of the cooling-room is generally reckoned as one-third of that of the cold store.

From the above calculations it is obvious that the size of a cold store can be exactly arrived at by figures guaranteed by experience. We must not, however, forget that the population for which the abattoir is to be built will be the basis to work on.

Capability of extension must not be disregarded, so that provision may be made for a possible increase in the consumption of meat from unforeseen causes. Such provision is best made by constructing a cellar under the whole of the cold store to be used in case of need. This reserve store will, however, not be supplied with refrigerating machinery and meat cells until absolute necessity requires it.

Hanging-House.

There can be no cold store without a hanging-house, if things are to be done in a proper manner. In the hanging-house the excess of animal heat is allowed to evaporate from the carcasses. If freshly-killed meat were brought straight into the cold store, aqueous vapour would develop in the cold temperature, as a person's breath condenses on a cold winter's day, the meat would become coated with damp, and the air, being surcharged with moisture, would lose its preservative power. At the best a hanging-house arranged in this way would be far more costly to manage.

The hanging-room must be well ventilated and roomy. In the cold store, on the other hand, every extra cubic inch of space must be saved in order to keep working expenses as low as possible.

It is not our intention to discuss the advantages and defects of the various refrigerating systems—the point we wish to insist on is that a cold store should be combined with the abattoir, and should be provided with cold dry air circulation.

Any town, moreover, which wishes to have the satisfactory working of its cold store guaranteed should only instal such refrigerating plant as long experience has proved to answer every requirement.

For conveying meat from the cold store to the butcher's shop a particular kind of meat-van is used in Germany, which has much to recommend it. In shape these vans resemble a furniture van, or an omnibus without windows, having, however, proper openings for ventilation.

Carcasses are hung at the sides of the van—not laid upon each other—and internal organs—liver, lungs, etc. —are suspended from movable hooks in the middle. The carcasses of animals from which the hide has not been removed—as, for instance, calves—may be laid on the floor of the van. The vehicle is hung very low, so that it can be easily entered, and has close-fitting doors at the back, and movable steps attached to facilitate the lifting of carcasses into the van. The inside is lined with zinc, so that it can be easily cleaned by washing.

These meat-vans are, of course, intended to carry meat in such a way that its appearance is not injured, as it would be by being packed in an ordinary cart, in which pieces of meat, instead of hanging as in the butcher's shop, are laid upon each other, and lose some of their freshness in transit.

TRANSLATOR'S NOTE.—This matter has been referred to in the first part of the book, English butchers complaining that abattoir-killed meat loses its 'bloom' by being carried from the abattoir to the shop. The German meat-van disposes of this objection.

THE ICE FACTORY.

If a cold store is attached to an abattoir there should undoubtedly be also an ice factory. To begin with, the manufacture of ice lessens the cost of the cold store as being a valuable product; and, secondly, service is at the same time rendered to the cause of hygiene. When we read the statements of bacteriologists as to the countless number of disease germs found in natural ice, we hail with satisfaction the production of artificial ice, which is free from bacilli. Even though artificial ice be not absolutely without germs, nor perfectly clear in appearance, still, if it be made from good drinking-water, the advantage gained is great.

In the newest abattoirs none but clear or 'crystal' ice, free from germs, is manufactured, on the principle that the abattoir should represent hygiene in every way. This kind of ice, made of pure distilled water, is the most perfect form of ice for human consumption procurable. By removing all air-bubbles from the water, the ice made is absolutely transparent and clear as crystal. The extraordinary amount of ice sold at the different abattoirs is sufficient proof of the great demand for ice of this description.

Ice is a by-product of the cold store, and the cost of its manufacture while the cold store is being worked is infinitesimal. Were it necessary to interfere with or suspend the working of the cold store while ice is being manufactured, the case would be different. The cost of ice-making would then be considerable. A system of compensation may be arranged by having reserve cellars cooled by refrigerating machinery, in which ice which has not been disposed of can be preserved, and this reserve store can be always drawn on in cold weather —*i.e.*, when the machinery for cooling the cold store would not be working. In many cases the whole amount of ice produced can be disposed of by contract to retail dealers, who thus supply the public with pure ice for preserving all kinds of provisions.

The Pickling-Room.

If much preserved meat is consumed in a town, it will be advisable to have proper rooms for preparing it in. The most important of these rooms is the pickling-room, while a smoking-room may be added. Very occasionally pickling-rooms require to be artificially cooled. If it is possible to have cellars under the cold store, the temperature of such cellars, if properly insulated, will not be more than 44° F., which is the best temperature for pickling.

If, however, cellars of this kind cannot be obtained, the pickling-room must be artificially cooled, so that, especially during hot weather, the meat kept there may not suffer.

In exceptional cases pickling-rooms are expensively fitted up. Walls faced with concrete are quite sufficient; the flooring is generally of asphalt. Various compartments are enclosed with wooden lattice (since the air impregnated with salt injures iron), the wood being varnished. The pickling-tanks are either of cement or earthenware, and the compartments in which they are placed are larger or smaller, according to local requirements. The smallest measure 10 feet square. They are generally shut off from the passages by sliding doors, which slide upwards to afford admission.

We must add that upon no consideration whatever should salt meat be kept in the cold store. This would cause the air to be saturated with moisture, having a most injurious effect on the meat stored there, and one most difficult to remedy.

Sausage-making Department.

The centralising of all work connected with slaughtering in one public establishment was in response to the general desire that the preparation of meat and the meat trade itself should be subject to proper control.

Such a desire is especially justified with regard to the manufacture of sausages. It is impossible to tell of what sausages may consist, however clean and attractive their appearance may be. It is therefore imperative that their manufacture should be subjected to supervision. As soon as a newly-built abattoir is opened the manufacture of sausages should be immediately transferred to it and carried on there. We wish to insist on the word *immediately*, for were the attempt made to take such a step after the lapse of several years, the greatest opposition would be met with.

The rooms in which these popular delicacies are prepared surpass, if possible, all other departments of the abattoir in the elegance of their appointments, and the manufacture is carried on under the direct supervision of the proper officials. Meat-mincing machines of the very latest patterns are employed, and driven by electric motors as required.

The carcasses which are to be worked up into sausages are laid out on clean maple-wood tables and carefully boned. The weight of the meat to be minced is then ascertained by the officials in charge, and the proper fee exacted.

Arrangements are also made for cooking and smoking sausages, and the rooms in which this is done are models of cleanliness and convenience. In cold weather these rooms are heated by stoves, and lavatories are provided

GERMAN SAUSAGE FACTORY.

with hot and cold water, so that the workmen may wash their hands before setting to work.

We need not add that materials for sausages prepared under such conditions need be regarded with no suspicion, and may be consumed without misgiving, which has not always been the case in the past.

The scrupulous cleanliness with which the manufacture of sausages is carried on, and which soon becomes a matter of public knowledge, helps to increase the demand for them both at home and abroad.

Fat and Tallow Rendering.

In order to avoid the nuisance of offensive smells, establishments for this kind of work are sometimes placed outside the town, and may be combined with the abattoir. Rooms are built in which the raw material can be stored until it is worked up; and public work-rooms are also created in which the fat is melted down.

In abattoirs the fat and tallow-melting department is always relegated to a remote position, and is generally placed near the boiler-house. The object of this is in order that the evil-smelling gases may be carried under the boiler fire and consumed without being noticed.

By a tallow-melting factory is meant one in which tallow is manufactured for various purposes. It has been said that by combining works of this kind with the abattoir, the production of good oleofat for margarine is greatly increased and the quality improved.

We append a few examples of the amount yielded in annual rents by establishments of this kind:

	£		£
In Krefeld ...	140	In Leipzig ...	173
,, Magdeburg...	244	,, Halle ...	104
,, Berlin ...	1,400	,, Brunswick ...	300
,, Breslau ...	175	,, Cologne ...	213
,, Barmen ...	70	,, Essen ...	166

Hide-storing Department.

The same objection on the score of bad smells, which holds in the case of melting down fat, also applies to the storing of hides in a town. The objection also is not confined to noxious smells, but also to the possible spread of infectious disease by the agency of insects.

The wish is, therefore, very naturally felt, as soon as an abattoir is built, that all hides should be stored there, instead of in the town.

The spacious lofts over the slaughtering-halls are especially used for drying hides. Drying-sheds are built as well in any out-of-the-way part of the abattoir, care being taken to have them thoroughly ventilated.

If the hides of slaughtered animals are merely to be salted, and then sent off from the abattoir, the building for storing them can be very simply constructed, as no fittings are required.

We will next discuss those supplementary buildings which, while not essential to an abattoir, are yet of great service, and which help to swell the income of the establishment.

Blood-drying Department.

Originally all blood not used for making sausages was allowed to flow away down the drains. It has now been discovered that, with a small amount of labour, blood may be made a source of considerable profit to the abattoir. The blood is collected, poured into vessels in which it is dried by steam and reduced to a powder.

This steaming and drying process renders any infectious matter which may be present in the blood perfectly innocuous. The product obtained is used as food-meal either by itself or in combination with molasses, the residuary product of sugar-refining.

The demand for this blood-meal is so great that makers of blood-drying plant offer to supply the necessary machinery to slaughter-houses free of charge if the manufactured product is delivered to them by truck-loads, under a contract for a certain number of years. After the lapse of the stipulated time the blood-drying establishments become the absolute property of the town, without any further compensation being paid. This fact warrants us in concluding that the profits made are considerable, and that it would be a mistake on the part of towns owning abattoirs not to retain these profits in their own hands.

Besides blood-drying establishments, albumin factories are found in modern abattoirs—albumin being a material used in calico-printing. Pepsine factories also are often built in abattoirs, as well as factories for coagulated blood prepared on the Kjär system, and tonic food on that of Huch.

Sausage-skin Cleaning Department.

In small abattoirs the sausage-skin cleaning is always done in the tripe-house. The intestines of slaughtered animals are made into sausage-skins by scraping the fat and outer tissue from them. In large establishments there is always a separate building for the cleaning, and this is especially necessary when, instead of the cleaning being done by the butchers themselves, the intestines are sold to a special class of dealers. This is the case in Alsace and South Germany, where the so-called 'Küttlers,' or tripe-dealers, purchase the heads, intestines, and fat of slaughtered animals, which they clean and prepare for food.

The skin-cleaning department makes a good return in the way of rent. At Leipzig the annual dues amount to £120; at Magdeburg to £92; at Berlin to as much as £956.

'Destructors' for consuming Carcasses.

Local requirements must decide whether a special building for the destruction by heat of meat unfit for food is added to the abattoir. In every abattoir proper arrangements should be made for the safe and thorough destruction of all confiscated meat. The hygienic character of the institution itself demands that this should be done. The chief agents required for working 'destructors'—namely, water, steam, and mechanical power—should all be available in an abattoir.

No doubt there is a certain prejudice against the presence of buildings of this description in an abattoir, as it seems to bring the business of the knacker into close connection with the work of the abattoir. But it must be remembered that, just as there are private slaughtering establishments whose arrangements are little superior to those of the knackers in country districts, so there are establishments for the destruction of unsound meat which in their internal appointments, cleanliness, etc., compare most favourably with the most modern abattoir.

Moreover, special care is always taken that a building of this kind in an abattoir shall be isolated as far as possible, that it shall have its own entrance giving access from outside, and that the staff of workmen employed in it shall do no work in the abattoir itself. In thickly-populated country districts, where villages are numerous, the authorities are strongly in favour of these establishments, in which carcasses are destroyed in the safest possible manner.

All 'destructors' resemble each other in the following points: The animal's carcass is placed in a large steam-proof cylinder, which can be hermetically closed, and there, by the application of steam under high pressure, reduced to bone-meal, fat, and glue. These products are subsequently separated from one another, and submitted to further processes of manufacture.

Special arrangements are made so that no annoyance is caused by unpleasant odours. Originally it was customary to dispose of all confiscated meat of a dangerous character by consuming it in the boiler furnace. A certain amount of fuel was required for this, and a certain amount of expense entailed. Modern destructors, on the other hand, require very little steam, destroying animal matter safely and without unpleasant odours; and although in some cases some additional expenditure is involved, this is quite compensated for by the great hygienic value of destroying infectious matter in a thoroughly reliable manner.

A small destructor establishment in Stolp brings in £106 yearly against an expenditure of £70, so that there is a clear profit of £36.

Of course, it is possible to have independent destructor establishments separate from any abattoir, but, as can be well understood, they are more profitably worked when combined with the public slaughter-house. When properly fitted up, their presence cannot be objected to in an abattoir, even from an æsthetic point of view.

Milk Inspection Department.

No place can be better fitted for the inspection of milk than the laboratory of an abattoir. Proper veterinary surgeons are on the spot, assisted by food analysts, who are employed to conduct accurate analyses of all kinds.

Questionable milk, suspected of adulteration, is examined in the laboratory, the number by which it is designated having been sent in, and in the shortest possible time the result of the analysis is submitted to the authorities.

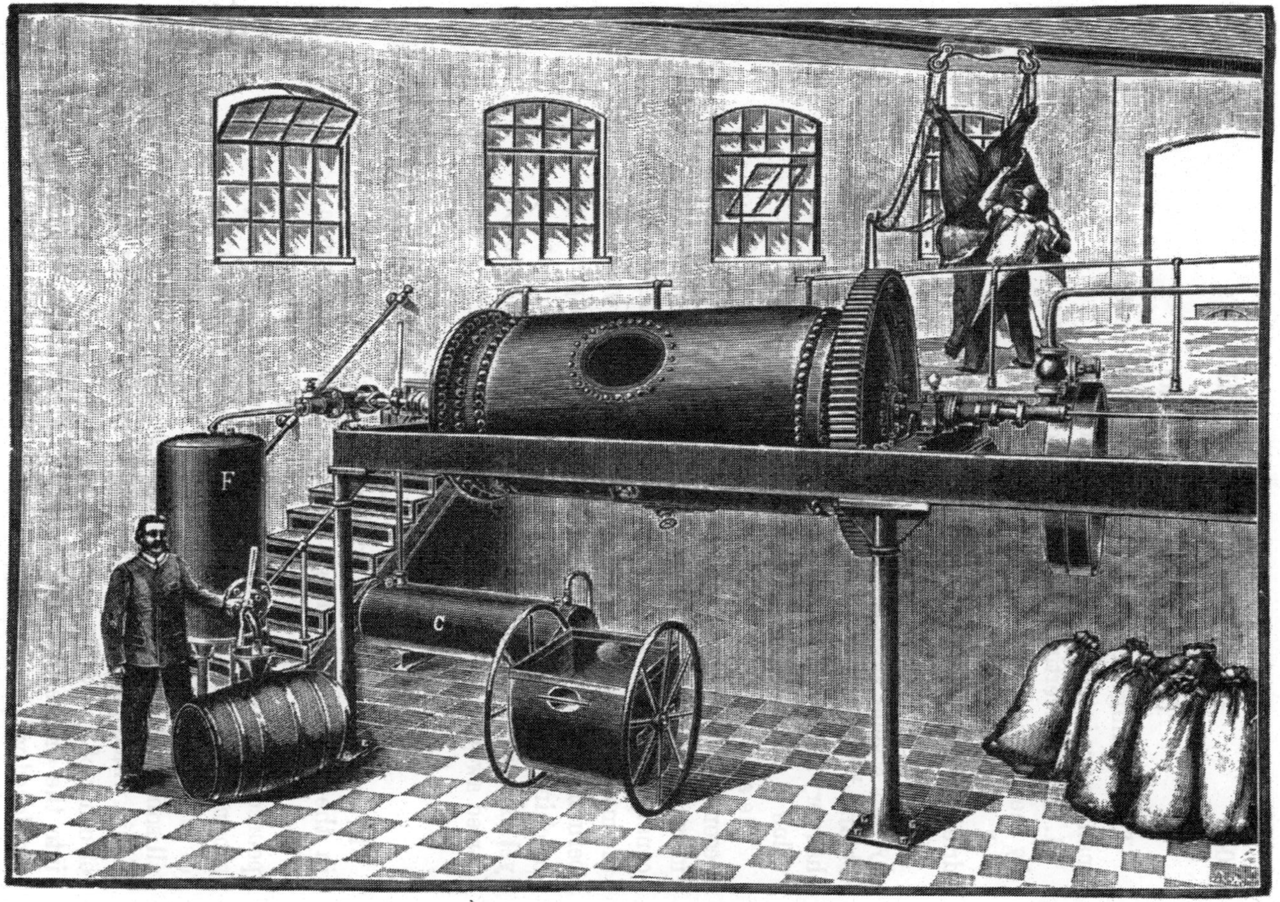

PODEWIL'S DESTRUCTOR.

The Utilisation of Manure.

The buildings erected in abattoirs for the treatment of manure are intended for a double purpose:

1. The converting of manure into fertilising powder by the addition of blood and other ingredients.
2. The manufacture of 'Briquettes,' which, when dried, may be used as fuel.

The manufacture of dry manure has been superseded by the second process described, because the manure obtained from the intestines of *large* animals, at any rate, has very little fertilising power, and is hardly of sufficient value to cover the cost of production.

The second system referred to has, on the other hand, become more popular, since the material in question forms excellent fuel, and after proper treatment can be consumed in the boiler furnace on the spot. Although the manufacture of the 'Briquettes' requires a workman permanently employed in moulding them in a pressing machine and afterwards placing them in drying-rooms, yet expense is saved because the manure has not to be carted away, but is used for fuel instead.

Purification of Sewage.

If an abattoir be not placed either on the banks of, or in the vicinity of, a large and rapidly-flowing stream, whose waters will carry off and disperse all sewage poured into it, it is absolutely necessary, on sanitary grounds, that arrangements be made for the purification of such sewage. By the construction of purifying works all solid matter which will not float is retained, while the liquid which passes on is purified and disinfected by one or other of the various systems employed before it flows into the drains or into a river. The particular system employed will largely depend on the volume of water in the river into which the sewage drains. In towns where the recently-introduced method of flushing drains is in vogue the purification of sewage is superfluous. The treatment of sewage will be much facilitated if the entrances to the drains in the various buildings are provided with the proper gullies, with gratings and 'grease-traps.' These gullies prevent large pieces of solid matter from entering the drains, and also check the accumulation of sludge in the clarifying tanks.

The different known systems for purifying sewage are:

1. The irrigation system.
2. Mechanical clarification.
3. Chemical-mechanical purification.
4. The bacterial system.
5. The electrical system.

The *irrigation system* answers well if there is ground in the vicinity of the abattoir suitable for a sewage-farm, although in some respects this system is not altogether to be recommended.

With regard to mere *mechanical clarification*, the process cannot be considered perfect, but is popular on account of its cheapness, and is in use at most abattoirs.

It does not completely cleanse the sewage-water, but to a certain extent eliminates the solid matter contained in it.

The process consists either in filtration or in the settling of floating matter.

Space forbids us, however, to discuss the merits of the various systems.

Perfect purification of sewage is attained if in addition to mechanical methods chemicals are employed to induce precipitation. The precipitants used for this purpose are lime, chloride of iron, alum, chlorine, argillaceous earth, and many others.

The many different processes in vogue may be gathered from the fact that no less than seventy-five precipitants are known and used. Of all these the most serviceable is lime. Sludge-pumps are always employed in sewage-works to remove accumulated deposits.

The process of *bacterial purification* has for its object to cause the bacteria which appear during the process of putrefaction and decomposition to alter the matter on which they feed by dissolving its combination with nitrogen. The end in view is to effect a chemical change in the sewage as regards its composition, so that no further decomposition may take place. This process is also known as oxidisation, and has been adopted at many abattoirs. The results obtained with it may be generally regarded as good, but it is at the same time the most costly to employ.

The *electrical process* must be referred to for the sake of completeness. For abattoirs, however, it is too expensive to be of practical use.

Home for Lost Dogs.

It is a very advisable measure, and one strongly recommended by societies for the prevention of cruelty to animals, to afford accommodation at the abattoir for lost dogs until they are either removed or destroyed. At the abattoir there are plenty of attendants to take charge of them temporarily, and also abundance of food. If the owners fail to appear, the animals are destroyed painlessly in a lethal chamber. This contrivance was invented in England by Dr. Ward Richardson, of London, and produces death painlessly by the agency of carbonic acid gas or chloroform.

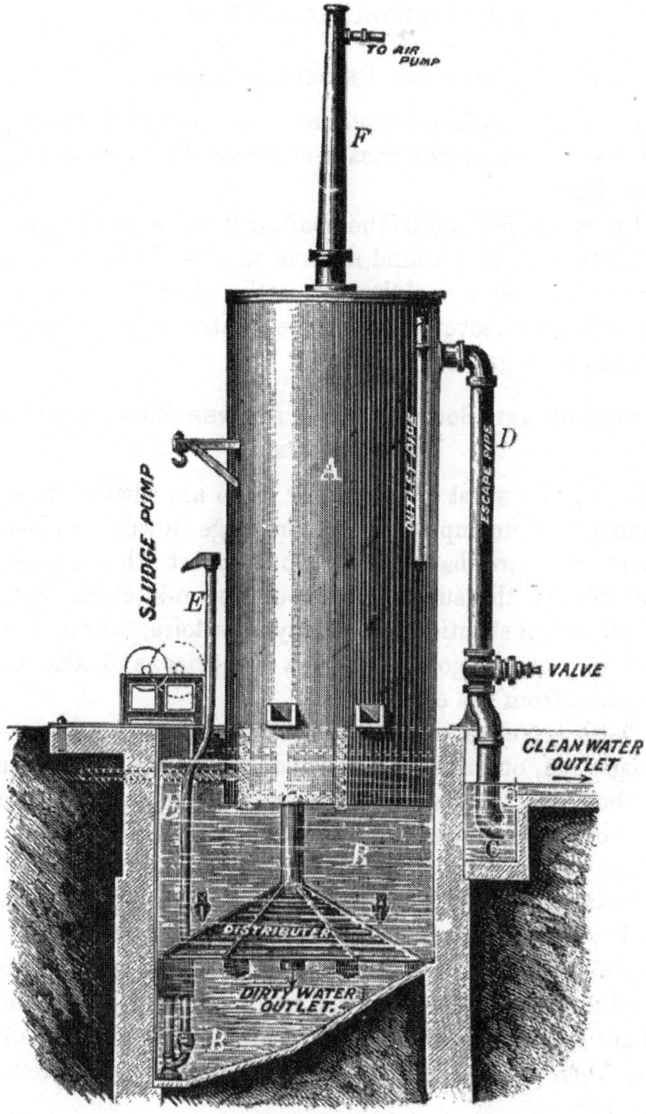
TO AIR PUMP
F
A
OUTLET PIPE
ESCAPE PIPE
D
SLUDGE PUMP
E
VALVE
CLEAN WATER OUTLET
C
E
R
DISTRIBUTER
DIRTY WATER OUTLET
B

SLUDGE-PUMP.

Factory for Preserved Meats.

In large abattoirs, especially in garrison towns, factories for preserved meats are built by the military authorities.

If they are situated in the abattoir there is an absolute certainty that only sound meat is used, and the work is done exclusively by soldiers on active duty. The meat inspection, moreover, is conducted entirely by military veterinary surgeons.

Sausage and Soup-Kitchens for the Poor, with Warm Shelters.

During the worst of the winter there are always large numbers of unemployed in our large towns, besides others who are barely able to support themselves. Societies for the support of popular soup-kitchens have established institutions in many abattoirs, where the poor may obtain good food at a low price, and also be sheltered from the cold.

These societies, whose philanthropic efforts deserve recognition, ought to be assisted by the municipalities in their efforts to alleviate distress. Rooms are placed at their disposal free of charge, generally in abattoirs where it is immaterial whether a room, more or less, is heated. Moreover, at the abattoir meat of inferior quality can be very cheaply purchased. The societies buy this meat as well as other portions of carcasses, such as the intestines, fat, etc., which are passed on to the poor. There is always a large supply of blood in an abattoir, and this can be worked up with bacon into cheap sausages.

Public Baths.

If there is no river-bathing to be had, and private bathing establishments are either wanting or unable to meet the demand, it is usual to have public shower-baths arranged at the abattoir. Such baths are very popular, and entail but slight expense, as there is always an abundant supply of hot and cold water to be had. The charge for their use is very low, and in many abattoirs the bath-rooms are most handsomely fitted up.

Management of the Abattoir.

In a modern abattoir the administrative authority, as we have mentioned, is vested in the veterinary surgeon, who is manager or director. He has his residence in the administrative block, is responsible to the municipality for the management of the abattoir, and has all other officials subordinated to him.

The financial (book-keeping) business of the abattoir is conducted by one or more clerks. It is their duty to issue tickets for the use of the abattoir, and to keep accounts.

The director controls the funds necessary for the management and working of the abattoir, within the limits of his budget, which must be so proportioned that the establishment can be always kept in good structural repair.

For the work of meat inspection, besides the chief official veterinary surgeon for the abattoir and district, subordinate inspectors may be appointed as required.

In towns all meat inspection is performed by veterinary surgeons, and their assistants merely help in the work of stamping, weighing, and inspecting for trichinosis.

The staff required for attending to cattle in the abattoir lairage, for keeping the buildings clean, and for looking after the establishment, varies according to the size of the abattoir.

Most of the staff will be lodged on the premises, so as

to be on the spot if required. Large abattoirs have their own engineers to superintend the machinery.

Working hours depend on local requirements. It is a principle, however, that no inspection can take place at night, nor can slaughtering be performed at night, except in cases of absolute necessity, or where the slaughtering-halls are perfectly illuminated with electric arc lights.

The length of the working hours greatly affects the income of the abattoir, and also, as we have said, the size of the slaughtering-rooms. It will be the object of the municipal authorities to shorten the hours as much as possible, and if this is to be done the matter should be settled as soon as the abattoir is opened.

The expenditure for steam, light, and water will be thus reduced to its utmost limits, and even with regard to the staff there will be a saving, as the men, if they are to work energetically, should never be on duty for more than ten consecutive hours. For longer hours a larger staff would have to be engaged and working expenses would increase.

With a view to the work being carried on in an orderly manner, it is forbidden to slaughter during the last hour before closing-time, so that every man has full time to finish whatever work he is engaged on. If slaughtering is done at any other than the regulation time a double fee is charged. By enforcing these rules, the butchers soon grow accustomed to orderly methods of business, and all the more readily because a reserve of meat for sale can always be kept in the cold store of the abattoir.

The time during which the cold store may be visited must also be regulated, in order to lessen working expenses, and cards of admission at a reasonable price—*e.g.*, sixpence—be issued. In this way things will be done in a business-like manner.

INSURANCE OF CATTLE.

In order to protect butchers from the loss they may incur through the confiscation of whole carcasses or parts of the same, the system of compulsory insurance has been introduced in most large abattoirs—a system which has given universal satisfaction to the butchers. It also greatly helps to reconcile butchers to compulsory slaughter and meat inspection.

In many states, for instance, Saxony, the system of compulsory insurance is universally established.

In Saxony no animal may be slaughtered before it has been notified as being insured. The payment of compensation follows immediately on the seizure of the carcass, and the money is handed over in the counting-house of the abattoir. This system has been heartily approved of on all hands, especially by the farming interest.

CONCLUSION.

We have now attempted to convey to our readers an accurate idea of the modern abattoir, to show what it is and what it does.

The illustrations of some of our best establishments, which accompany the text, bring out plainly the vast difference between slaughtering operations in a modern abattoir with the latest appliances, and the old system of private slaughter-houses. The results achieved have been the outcome of experience dearly bought, and those results are now placed at the service of other countries in the interests of public hygiene.

The object kept in view in modern abattoirs is to meet every requirement of modern sanitation in the minutest details, and that object is actually realised. Care is taken that no dweller in a town shall suffer the least annoyance either from actual slaughtering operations or from any causes connected therewith; that there shall be no pollution either of soil or river-water through slaughter-house refuse; that no suspicion of any kind shall attach to meat as an article of diet; that there shall be no possibility of unsound meat being offered for sale, and that, if it be not immediately destroyed, it shall be preserved in such a way as to comply with every sanitary requirement; that, finally, in the processes of meat-mincing and preserving, the highest possible standard of cleanliness shall be observed.

If, throughout the present work, we have continually kept the condition of things in Germany before the reader's view, we must plead in justification the wide experience enjoyed by Germany in this particular field. Not only does the building of public slaughter-houses in this country date back many centuries, but during the last thirty years there has been such development of the public slaughter-house system that at the present moment the German abattoir stands as a model for the world to imitate.

THE END

BILLING AND SONS, LTD., PRINTERS, GUILDFORD